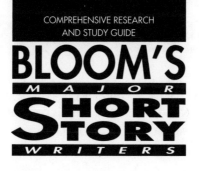

COMPREHENSIVE RESEARCH
AND STUDY GUIDE

BLOOM'S
MAJOR
SHORT STORY
WRITERS

F. Scott
Fitzgerald

EDITED AND WITH AN
INTRODUCTION BY HAROLD BLOOM

CURRENTLY AVAILABLE

BLOOM'S MAJOR DRAMATISTS

Anton Chekhov
Henrik Ibsen
Arthur Miller
Eugene O'Neill
Shakespeare's Comedies
Shakespeare's Histories
Shakespeare's Romances
Shakespeare's Tragedies
George Bernard Shaw
Tennessee Williams

BLOOM'S MAJOR NOVELISTS

Jane Austen
The Brontës
Willa Cather
Charles Dickens
William Faulkner
F. Scott Fitzgerald
Nathaniel Hawthorne
Ernest Hemingway
Toni Morrison
John Steinbeck
Mark Twain
Alice Walker

BLOOM'S MAJOR SHORT STORY WRITERS

William Faulkner
F. Scott Fitzgerald
Ernest Hemingway
O. Henry
James Joyce
Herman Melville
Flannery O'Connor
Edgar Allan Poe
J. D. Salinger
John Steinbeck
Mark Twain
Eudora Welty

BLOOM'S MAJOR WORLD POETS

Geoffrey Chaucer
Emily Dickinson
John Donne
T. S. Eliot
Robert Frost
Langston Hughes
John Milton
Edgar Allan Poe
Shakespeare's Poems & Sonnets
Alfred, Lord Tennyson
Walt Whitman
William Wordsworth

BLOOM'S NOTES

The Adventures of Huckleberry Finn
Aeneid
The Age of Innocence
Animal Farm
The Autobiography of Malcolm X
The Awakening
Beloved
Beowulf
Billy Budd, Benito Cereno, & Bartleby the Scrivener
Brave New World
The Catcher in the Rye
Crime and Punishment
The Crucible

Death of a Salesman
A Farewell to Arms
Frankenstein
The Grapes of Wrath
Great Expectations
The Great Gatsby
Gulliver's Travels
Hamlet
Heart of Darkness & The Secret Sharer
Henry IV, Part One
I Know Why the Caged Bird Sings
Iliad
Inferno
Invisible Man
Jane Eyre
Julius Caesar

King Lear
Lord of the Flies
Macbeth
A Midsummer Night's Dream
Moby-Dick
Native Son
Nineteen Eighty-Four
Odyssey
Oedipus Plays
Of Mice and Men
The Old Man and the Sea
Othello
Paradise Lost
A Portrait of the Artist as a Young Man
The Portrait of a Lady

Pride and Prejudice
The Red Badge of Courage
Romeo and Juliet
The Scarlet Letter
Silas Marner
The Sound and the Fury
The Sun Also Rises
A Tale of Two Cities
Tess of the D'Urbervilles
Their Eyes Were Watching God
To Kill a Mockingbird
Uncle Tom's Cabin
Wuthering Heights

COMPREHENSIVE RESEARCH
AND STUDY GUIDE

BLOOM'S
MAJOR
SHORT
STORY
WRITERS

F. Scott
Fitzgerald

© 1999 by Chelsea House Publishers, a division of Main Line Book Co.

Introduction © 1999 by Harold Bloom

Printed and bound in the United States of America.

3 5 7 9 8 6 4 2

ISBN: 0-7910-5122-6

Library of Congress Cataloging-in-Publication Data applied for

Chelsea House Publishers
1974 Sproul Road, Suite 400
Broomall, PA 19008-0914

Contributing Editor: Pearl James

Contents

User's Guide

This volume is designed to present biographical, critical, and bibliographical information on the author's best-known or most important short stories. Following Harold Bloom's editor's note and introduction is a detailed biography of the author, discussing major life events and important literary accomplishments. A plot summary of each short story follows, tracing significant themes, patterns, and motifs in the work, and an annotated list of characters supplies brief information on the main characters in each story.

A selection of critical extracts, derived from previously published material from leading critics, analyzes aspects of each short story. The extracts consist of statements from the author, if available, early reviews of the work, and later evaluations up to the present. A bibliography of the author's writings (including a complete list of all books written, cowritten, edited, and translated), a list of additional books and articles on the author and the work, and an index of themes and ideas in the author's writings conclude the volume.

~

Harold Bloom is Sterling Professor of the Humanities at Yale University and Henry W. and Albert A. Berg Professor of English at the New York University Graduate School. He is the author of over 20 books and the editor of more than 30 anthologies of literary criticism.

Professor Bloom's works include *Shelley's Mythmaking* (1959), *The Visionary Company* (1961), *Blake's Apocalypse* (1963), *Yeats* (1970), *A Map of Misreading* (1975), *Kabbalah and Criticism* (1975), and *Agon: Toward a Theory of Revisionism* (1982). *The Anxiety of Influence* (1973) sets forth Professor Bloom's provocative theory of the literary relationships between the great writers and their predecessors. His most recent books include *The American Religion* (1992), *The Western Canon* (1994), *Omens of Millennium: The Gnosis of Angels, Dreams, and Resurrection* (1996), and *Shakespeare: The Invention of the Human* (1998).

Professor Bloom earned his Ph.D. from Yale University in 1955 and has served on the Yale faculty since then. He is a 1985 MacArthur Foundation Award recipient and served as the Charles Eliot Norton Professor of Poetry at Harvard University in 1987-88. He is currently the editor of other Chelsea House series in literary criticism, including BLOOM'S NOTES, BLOOM'S MAJOR POETS, MAJOR LITERARY CHARACTERS, MODERN CRITICAL VIEWS, MODERN CRITICAL INTERPRETATIONS, and WOMEN WRITERS OF ENGLISH AND THEIR WORKS.

Editor's Note

My Introduction relates Scott Fitzgerald's short stories to the John Keats of the Great Odes and the epic fragments.

As there are some thirty critical views, I will indicate only what I judge to be some of the high points. Malcolm Cowley on "May Day" clarifies Fitzgerald's financial obsessions, while Arthur Mizener sets the story in relation to social history.

On the fantastic "The Diamond as Big as the Ritz," Charles Weir, Jr., emphasizes class distinctions, while Marius Bewley invokes the sorrows of the "American Dream," and Lawrence Buell expounds the story's subtle representation of temporality.

"Babylon Revisited" is elucidated in Hawthornean terms by Roy R. Male, after which Carlos Baker disentangles the tale's thematic complexities.

Ellen Moers describes Fitzgerald's equivocal relation to Hollywood in "Crazy Sunday," while Kenneth Eble establishes the actual persons and events that are refracted in the story.

Introduction

HAROLD BLOOM

If Ernest Hemingway was the Lord Byron of our century, Scott Fitzgerald is one of the prime candidates for our John Keats. Hemingway and Fitzgerald were close friends, unlike Byron and Keats, but despite the affinities between *The Sun Also Rises* and *The Great Gatsby*, the short stories by the two writers diverge greatly—in mode, stance, and style, though not always in theme. Both Hemingway and Fitzgerald stemmed in part from the novelistic procedures of Joseph Conrad, but their American precursors were very different. Hemingway acknowledged the Mark Twain of *Huckleberry Finn*, though stylistically the poetry of his prose owed much to Walt Whitman, perhaps without self-awareness. Fitzgerald turned to Henry James and Edith Wharton, whose societal contexts suited his own dreams of wealth and his Keatsian nostalgia for lost erotic possibilities.

Though *Tender Is the Night* (its title from "The Ode to a Nightingale") opens beautifully, Fitzgerald's major novel is both uneven and self-indulgent, and the unfinished *The Last Tycoon* is of mixed aesthetic quality. After *The Great Gatsby,* the best of Fitzgerald is in many of the short stories, including the four examined in this volume. As with Keats's odes and epic fragments, Fitzgerald's stories and novels are parables of election, of achieving or failing the severe tests of the imagination, which is seen as a power profoundly capable of destruction. "May Day" ends with Gordon Sterrett's suicide, a failed artist passing a last judgment upon himself at the age of twenty-four. A grand fantasy, "The Diamond as Big as the Ritz," achieves closure by accepting "the shabby gift of disillusion," with its protagonist urging a "divine drunkenness" upon his paramour: "let us love for a while, for a year or two, you and me." Keats's affirmation of "the holiness of the heart's affections" is not mocked, but certainly it has been distanced.

In its high artistry, "Babylon Revisited" surpasses even *The Great Gatsby,* and compares well with Hemingway's strongest stories. Babylon is not so much Paris (in the days of Gertrude Stein and Hemingway) as it is A.E. Housman's "land of lost content." Charlie

Wales, a Fitzgerald-surrogate, is more punished than his minor sins deserve. Widowed and deprived of his daughter, Wales evokes authentic pathos and suffers nostalgia and regret. A kind of elegy for the Lost Generation, "Babylon Revisited" is as adroit and balanced in style as Keats's odes and Hemingway's stories, which hover near, yet at a precise aesthetic distance.

Fitzgerald's final phase, his Hollywood years, is exemplified by "Crazy Sunday," the most finished story to emerge from those years of decline. Keats's dialectic of creation and destroying governs "Crazy Sunday," where Miles Calman pays for his art by doom-eagerness, and Joel Coles drifts towards the loss of self. The high theatricality of Stella Walker Calman is the culmination of Fitzgerald's visions of a fatal Muse, including not only Daisy in *The Great Gatsby* and Nicole in *Tender Is the Night*, but the formidable Zelda Fitzgerald herself, the last of the belles. ❀

Biography of
F. Scott Fitzgerald

(1896–1940)

Francis Scott Key Fitzgerald was born in 1896 in St. Paul, Minnesota, to Edward and Mary McQuillan Fitzgerald. His mother's family were Irish immigrants who came to the United States during the Great Famine of the 1840s and ran a profitable grocery business in St. Paul. Although Mary inherited a good living, the Fitzgerald family had difficulty maintaining the high standard of middle-class life to which they had been bred. His father was born in Maryland and could trace his maternal roots to the colonial period and to such famous ancestors as Scott's namesake, Francis Scott Key, who wrote "The Star Spangled Banner." A sister, Annabel, was born in 1901. The family lived in Buffalo and in Syracuse, New York, but eventually settled permanently in St. Paul.

F. Scott Fitzgerald showed literary talent at an early age. He kept a written record of his early impressions and experiences and developed his ability as a keen social observer. As a teenager he wrote mysteries for his school paper and plays for amateur productions.

His parents eventually sent him to the Newman School in New Jersey, a small Catholic preparatory school. There, he struggled for (but never quite achieved) popularity and continued with his writing. He formed a strong attachment to a priest, Father Sigourney Fay, a well-educated and cultured man. Father (later Monsignor) Fay encouraged his interest in literature and was a role model when Fitzgerald briefly considered entering the priesthood.

From the Newman School, Fitzgerald went to Princeton University. He loved Princeton's privileged atmosphere and its Gothic architecture, but he was not a particularly good student. He dreamed of being a football star, but at five feet seven inches, he lacked the size. He continued to write stories, poems, plays, and song lyrics and was involved in several dramatic productions of the Princeton Triangle Club; poor grades, however, made it difficult for him to participate as much as he would have liked. He formed lasting friendships with the poet and novelist John Peale Bishop and the critic Edmund

Wilson, both of whom shared his interest in literature and exerted strong influence on his development as a reader. He fell in love with a debutante, Ginevra King, and enjoyed a lively social life of dances, parties, and visits. Poor study habits and poor health forced Fitzgerald to take a leave of absence and to forfeit the presidency of the Cottage Club and a performance in a Triangle show he had co-written—all long-felt disappointments.

When the United States entered the First World War, in 1917, Fitzgerald enlisted and received a commission as an infantry second lieutenant. While in training, he spent his weekends working on his first novel, *The Romantic Egoist.* Stationed near Montgomery, Alabama, he attended a dance and met Zelda Sayre, a wild-spirited, fun-loving, spoiled, beautiful girl—the last child born to a judge and his wife. Like Fitzgerald, Zelda was ambitious and wanted more than life in Montgomery could offer. Soon they were in love.

The war ended before Fitzgerald's unit was sent abroad (another disappointment). Discharged in 1919, he went to New York to make his fortune and earn Zelda's hand. But after a few tedious months in the advertising business, some serious drinking bouts, and painful rejections from publishers for his writing, it seemed that he and Zelda would not be able to marry. She broke off their engagement, and Fitzgerald went home to St. Paul, where he revised his novel.

That fall, *This Side of Paradise* was accepted, he published several stories, and he found a literary agent, Harold Ober. In 1920, he and Zelda were married in New York. *This Side of Paradise* was an immediate success, and the Fitzgeralds became the dashing and wild young stars of an exuberant, fashionable social scene. They moved to France in the early 1920s to live among a circle of American expatriate writers that included Ernest Hemingway and Gertrude Stein.

Scott and Zelda Fitzgerald shared a penchant for excess—financial, alcoholic, and emotional—that made their adult married life tumultuous, exciting, and difficult. They traveled much, living in hotels and rented flats and houses in Europe and New York; occasionally, they returned to St. Paul or Montgomery, to be near their parents. Their daughter, Scottie, was born in 1921.

Fitzgerald wrote and sold short stories for considerable sums of money, all the while struggling to find the time to finish his novels, which required long periods of concentrated work. *The Beautiful and Damned* appeared in 1922 to some critical and financial success. His greatest novel, *The Great Gatsby*, was published in 1925. *Gatsby* did not sell well commercially but was recognized by critics as a masterpiece. Between novels, his publisher, Charles Scribner, collected the short stories, some of which were also marketed to the film studios in Hollywood. His next novel, *Tender Is the Night*, took several years to finish, and was not published until 1934.

Zelda Fitzgerald wrote, danced, and painted, but allowed her artistic talents to take a back seat to her husband's. She suffered the first of several mental and emotional breakdowns in 1930. Scott drank heavily, which exacerbated his inability to cope with her illness; their economic imprudence also made things difficult. By 1934, Zelda was being hospitalized for longer and longer periods; Scottie's upbringing was left in the hands of family, friends, and the child's boarding school. (Zelda eventually died in a fire at the Highland Sanitarium, near Ashville, North Carolina, in 1947.)

In 1937, Fitzgerald's financial debts to his agent and his publisher forced him to seek work in Hollywood as a screenwriter for the Metro-Goldwyn-Mayer studio. The work was dull and frustrating; he took out his bitterness in a series of satirical stories about a hack writer named Pat Hobby. He met Sheila Graham, another Hollywood screenwriter, who became his companion. His drinking, still a problem, was more controlled than it had been for the past fifteen years.

F. Scott Fitzgerald died of a heart attack in 1940, while working on his fifth novel, *The Last Tycoon*. It was published posthumously, as were collections of his stories and essays. In the 1960s his work received new attention, and his literary reputation as a major American writer was assured. ❀

Plot Summary of
"May Day"

"May Day" first appeared in the magazine *The Smart Set* in July 1920 and was subsequently included in Fitzgerald's second collection of short stories, *Tales of the Jazz Age* (1922). Critics have consistently praised it as one of Fitzgerald's most mature and ambitious efforts. The story takes place on May 1 (May Day, the holiday for radical labor), 1919, a date historically significant for its outbreaks of anti-radical violence and riots in several American cities that marked the beginning of a yearlong Red scare. Fitzgerald brings this tumultuous moment in American history into focus through a small but interlocking group of characters.

"May Day" has an unusually wide scope for a short story (Fitzgerald originally envisioned it as a novel). It is composed of eleven sections introduced by a breezy, satirical narrator. Whether these sections form an artistic whole is debatable. The narrator raises the question himself, in the introduction: "So during all this time there were many adventures that happened in the big city, and, of these, several—or perhaps one—are here set down." Fitzgerald brings together different characters to show the connection between different social worlds; the divisions seem too great, however, and the author's attempts to establish links between the fraternity ball at Delmonico's and the riot at the *New York Trumpet* ring false. Nevertheless, several themes that Fitzgerald explores elsewhere in his work also unify this story: the gaps between the rich, the poor, and the in-between; prematurely jaded youth; the lure and effects of alcohol; and the artist brought low by a woman.

The story begins when Gordon Sterrett, a struggling and, perhaps, not very talented artist, comes to visit Philip Dean, a college friend, recently arrived in New York. As Sterrett waits in Dean's hotel room while Dean dresses, Fitzgerald details the visible differences in their economic conditions. The "thick silk shirts littered on the chairs" in Dean's room represent financial excess (items of value are "littered"), in contrast with Sterrett's current poverty. As he takes stock of "his own shirt-cuffs," which are "ragged and linty at the edges and soiled to a faint gray," Sterrett thinks, "quite without amusement, that only three years before he had received a scattering vote in the senior elections at college for being the best-dressed man in his class."

Fitzgerald implies here that the old adage is true: Clothes make the man. Sterrett's "well-cut, shabby suit" marks him as a man in decline: he has lost his job, fallen prey to a woman who is no longer "pure," and is in the process of losing his place in the world.

The material and external signs of Sterrett's fall precisely correspond to the state of his spirit:

> Dean scrutinized him more closely with appraising blue eyes.
> "You certainly look all shot."
> "I am. I've made a hell of a mess of everything."

The relationship between appearance and reality that Fitzgerald emphasizes is not yet obvious, ironically, to Sterrett himself, who mistakenly thinks that his friendship with Dean—maybe even his romance with Edith Bradin—goes deeper and means more than his current misfortunes. But as the economic gap widens between them, Dean's and Sterrett's relationship changes. Dean's initial enthusiasm for "Gordy" dies and is replaced by a much stronger emotion when Sterrett asks him for money, "for in that instant they quite suddenly and definitely hated each other."

Sterrett's fall, made "irrevocable" by his suicide (and not, as he thinks, by his marriage to Jewel) seems incommensurate with his age—he is only twenty-four years old. But youth has already passed him by. The 1920s culture of youth that Fitzgerald flamboyantly lived and popularized in his writing is characterized by this sense of premature aging, of ennui. This idle boredom unites most of the characters, transcending class distinctions. Sterrett, Edith Bradin, and the soldiers Carrol Key and Gus Rose all seem, in different ways, past their prime. Their futures are variously vague and empty. Edith Bradin, the beautiful debutante at the ball at Delmonico's, thinks of love and marriage, but her self-absorption stands in the way of both. She no longer finds satisfaction in balls and parties, and out of boredom—or desire for adventure—or both—she decides to surprise her brother at the *New York Trumpet.*

In a daring coincidence, Fitzgerald draws a comparison between this young debutante and the debauched soldiers, Rose and Key: they, too, become involved in the riot out of boredom and happenstance. Fitzgerald undermines the political significance of the riots; certainly, Rose and Key have no political convictions. They have nothing to do and nowhere in particular to go, so they get drunk in the hope of passing time.

Their desire for alcohol provides another point of connection between the soldiers and their social superiors. Although initially Key and Rose have to hide in a back room of Delmonico's and drink surreptitiously, it is not long before Peter Himmel invites them to join the party. Himmel fought in the First World War himself, but as an officer. His quest for inebriation also stems from boredom and worry:

> At the second highball, boredom, disgust, the monotony of time, the turbidity of events, sank into a vague background before which glittering cobwebs formed. . . . With the departure of worry came brilliant, permeating symbolism. . . . He himself became in a measure symbolic . . . the brilliant dreamer at play.

In this description, Fitzgerald represents the lure that alcohol has for his characters in terms analogous to art itself. Alcohol gives conversation and events an air of meaning—something that "May Day" itself is constructed to do. As he drinks, Himmel feels himself becoming heroic and vainly imagines himself a dreamer, an artist figure. He is, however, increasingly an object of satire.

The story continually pairs characters as doubles. When Peter Himmel and Philip Dean become doubles for Rose and Key, the detrimental effects of alcohol become clear. The hilarity of their adventures as Mr. In and Mr. Out is only apparent to Himmel and Dean. If they are amused, it is at their own expense. When Rose and Key meet Himmel, they laugh "uproariously"; they laugh at him, not with him. For "to them a man who talked after this fashion was either raving drunk or raving crazy."

In "May Day," Fitzgerald suggests that there is not much difference between "raving drunk" and "raving crazy." Both states are potentially lethal. With the mob's violent attack on the *New York Trumpet* and with Sterrett's suicide, Fitzgerald shows that boredom and despair are kindred emotions, leading to equally dangerous conclusions.

Gordon Sterrett's suicide brings the story full circle. His weakness has made him a victim to Jewel Hudson, to whom he is now "irrevocably married." Jewel Hudson is one of the more interesting touches in "May Day." She is not entirely unsympathetic, and she may feel real emotion for Sterrett. (She explains that she did not start "bothering" Sterrett for money until he began "neglecting" her.) Her willfulness contrasts sharply with Sterrett's unmanly weakness. Unlike Sterrett, an artist of uncertain talent lacking in ambition, Jewel

Hudson knows what she wants and goes after it. By yielding to Jewel, Sterrett has lost hope. Jewel represents the world of both sensuality and domesticity that are death for the artist. "May Day" is one of the earliest examples of the danger that women pose to men, a theme that recurs throughout Fitzgerald's writing. ❀

List of Characters in
"May Day"

Gordon Sterrett graduated from Yale a few years before the First World War, moved to New York City, and has been unsuccessful in his dream of becoming an illustrator. He is down on his luck, having both lost his job and become involved with the wrong sort of woman. His hopelessness culminates in his suicide at the end of the story.

Philip Dean, a former classmate of Sterrett's, is in New York for a visit and to attend a party given by a college fraternity. He has enough family money to travel and to live a dissipated life, without worry for the future. He represents the standard of masculine success against which Gordon Sterrett's failure can be measured: He is healthy, well dressed, carefree.

Edith Bradin, a beautiful 22-year-old debutante, has begun to tire of her social routine of parties and balls. Impeccably dressed, a good dancer, adept at flirtatious conversation, she is bored and ready for adventure—within certain limits. Although she feels "made for love," she cannot love an unsuccessful man like Gordon Sterrett. On a whim, she leaves the party at Delmonico's unescorted and goes in search of her brother at his nearby office. There she witnesses the riot.

Henry Bradin, Edith's older brother, is an idealist. Having graduated from Cornell a few years before the war, he is of the same generation as Sterrett and Dean. Rather than attending college parties, however, Bradin pursues his political convictions and works late for a radical newspaper, the *New York Trumpet.* Ironically, his leg is broken by a group of rioters whose political interests he is trying to represent.

Peter Himmel offends his date, Edith Bradin, on the way to the dance at Delmonico's by trying to kiss her in the taxicab and inadvertently mussing her hair. Out of her favor, he spends the evening getting drunk and having a series of adventures with Philip Dean. He and Dean become "Mr. In" and "Mr. Out" when they take the restaurant's door signs and insert them in their shirt fronts.

Carrol Key, a recently discharged soldier, is adrift in New York City. Contrary to what the wartime rhetoric of the story's introduction suggests, there is nothing heroic about Key or his companion-in-arms, Gus Rose. Key and Rose are "ugly, ill-nourished, devoid of all except the very lowest form of intelligence." Key and Rose go to Delmonico's in search of Key's older brother, who may be willing to provide them with liquor illegally. After hiding in a back room for a while, the two ex-soldiers are discovered by Peter Himmel, and the three get drunk. Back on the street, Key and Rose join a mob and become part of the assault on the *New York Trumpet* offices. Key falls to his death during the riot. (Why Francis Scott Key Fitzgerald shares his own middle name with his character Carrol Key is an intriguing question.)

Gus Rose is the shorter counterpart to Carrol Key. Also a recent discharge, he is equally adrift and aimless. At the end of the story, Edith Bradin identifies him as one of the participants in the riot. Although he does not die in the riot, as Key does, he probably will face criminal charges.

Jewel Hudson is the "over-rouged" young woman who has become involved with Gordon Sterrett, much to his chagrin. Although Sterrett presents her to Dean as no longer "pure," and as an extortionist, she demonstrates some concern for him when she seeks him out at Delmonico's. Her independent spirit contrasts with the "weak-chinned" waiter at the party and with the weak-willed Gordon Sterrett. Although she is, like Edith Bradin, an assertive and self-possessed woman, she does not belong to the social world of debutante balls and fraternity parties. In the final section of the story, realizing that he is "irrevocably married" to Jewel, Sterrett decides to take his own life. ❀

Critical Views on
"May Day"

PAUL ROSENFELD ON DISILLUSIONED YOUTH

[Paul Rosenfeld (1890–1946) was a novelist and a critic of both music and literature. In this excerpt from *Men Seen: Twenty-Four Modern Authors* (1925), he considers the theme of disillusioned youth in "May Day."]

It is fresh, juicy and spontaneous that the American juvenile of the class described by Fitzgerald exactly are not. Superficially, perhaps. But was not the forest green which Europe called by the name of youth somewhat more a thing of courage? And the number of us willing to face the world without the panoply of elaborate material protections is not overwhelming. . . .

The spirit of the business world is established well before the advent of puberty; and the spirit of business is compromise, which is not exactly it would seem the spirit of youth.

And even the lightest, least satirical of Fitzgerald's pages bear testimonial to the prevalence of the condition. A moralist could gather evidence for a most terrible condemnation of bourgeois America from the books of this protagonist of youth. And yet, *Lieb Vaterland, magst ruhig sein.* It is not a state of immorality in the general sense of the word that might be uncovered. If by morality we mean obedience to the mores of the tribal, then Fitzgerald's diverting flappers and slickers are in no sense licentious. By means of necking parties and booze fights of the sort he describes the republic is maintained. Business rests on them. But immorality may be taken to signify a falling away from the ideal spirit of life, and in that sense America is proven the breeding ground of a kind of decay. In all unconsciousness Fitzgerald shows us types of poor golden young too shallow to feel, vainly attitudinizing in the effort to achieve sensation: girls who know they cannot live without riches and men perpetually sucking the bottle for solace. The people aren't young: they are merely narcissistic. Knowledge of life is gotten from books, and the naïveté is not quite lovely. That is all very well; one has not fault to find with it; it is quite sanitary and not at all messy as passion usually is; but why call it spring? And occasionally Fitzgerald drops the light guitar and with cool ferocity speaks the veritable name. *May Day*, perhaps the most mature of all his tales, brings the bitter brackish dry taste of decay fully to the mouth. . . .

The amusing insolence of his earlier manner of writing has persistently given way before a bolder, sharper stroke less personal in reference. The descriptions in *May Day*: the sight of the avenues, the drinking scene in Delmonico's, the adventures of Mr. In and Out, are done with quiet virtuosity. . . . And still, in spite of *May Day*, Fitzgerald has not yet crossed the line that bounds the field of art. He has seen his material from its own point of view, and he has seen it completely from without. But he has never done what the artist does: seen it simultaneously from within and without; and loved it and judged it, too. For *May Day* lacks a focal point, and merely juxtaposes a number of small pieces. Should Fitzgerald finally break his mold, and free himself of the compulsions of the civilization in which he grew, it might go badly with his popularity. It will be a pathetic story he will have to tell, the legend of a moon which never rose; and that is precisely the story a certain America does not wish to hear. Nevertheless, we would like hugely to hear him tell it. And Fitzgerald might scarcely miss his following.

—Paul Rosenfeld, *Men Seen: Twenty-Four Modern Authors* (New York: Charles Scribner's Sons, 1925):, pp. 73–76.

MALCOLM COWLEY ON FITZGERALD AND MONEY

[Malcolm Cowley (1898–1989), an eminent man of letters, wrote widely on American literature, on Fitzgerald, and the Jazz Age. His books include *Exile's Return* (1934) and *A Second Flowering: Works and Days of the Lost Generation* (1973). He edited *The Stories of F. Scott Fitzgerald* (1957) and *Fitzgerald and the Jazz Age* (1966). In this extract, he situates Fitzgerald's attitude towards money.]

There was one respect in which Fitzgerald, much as he regarded himself as a representative figure of the age, was completely different from most of its serious writers. In that respect he was, as I said, much closer to the men of his college year who were trying to get ahead in the business would; like them he was fascinated by the process of earning and spending money. The young businessmen of his time, much more than those of a later generation, had been taught to measure success, failure, and even virtue in pecuniary terms. They had learned in school and Sunday school that virtue was rewarded with money and vice punished by the loss of money; apparently their one aim should be to earn lots of it fast. Yet money was only a convenient and inadequate symbol for what they dreamed of earning. The best of them were like Jay Gatsby in having "some heightened sensitivity to the promise of life"; or they were like another Fitzgerald hero, Dexter Green of "Winter Dreams," who "wanted not association with glittering things and glittering people—he wanted the glittering things themselves." Their real dream was that of achieving a new status and a new essence, of rising to a loftier place in the mysterious hierarchy of human worth.

The serious writers also dreamed of rising to a loftier status, but—except for Fitzgerald—they felt that moneymaking was the wrong way to rise. [. . .]

In his attitude toward money he revealed the new spirit of an age when conspicuous accumulation was giving way to conspicuous earning and spending. It was an age when gold was melted down and became fluid; when wealth was no longer measured in possessions—land, house, livestock, machinery—but rather in dollars per year, as a stream is measured by its flow; when for the first time the expenses of government were being met by income taxes more than by property and excise taxes; and when the new tax structure was making it somewhat more difficult to accumulate a stable and lasting fortune. Such fortunes still existed at the hardly accessible peak of the social system, which young men dreamed of reaching like Alpinists, but the romantic figures of the age were not capitalists properly speaking. They were salaried executives and advertising men, they were promoters, salesmen, stock gamblers, or racketeers, and they were millionaires in a new sense—not men each of whom owned a million dollars' worth of property, but men who lived in rented apartments and had nothing but stock certificates and insurance policies (or nothing but credit and the right connections), while spending more than the income of the old millionaires.

The change went deep into the texture of American society and deep into the feelings of Americans as individuals. Fitzgerald is its most faithful recorder, not only in the stories that earned him a place in the new high-income class, but also in his personal confessions. He liked to describe his vitality and his talent in pecuniary terms.

—Malcolm Cowley, *A Second Flowering* (New York: Scribner's, 1956): pp. 61, 63.

ARTHUR MIZENER ON FITZGERALD AND HISTORY

[Arthur Mizener (1907–1988) was a professor of literature at Yale and Cornell universities. In addition to several other books, he wrote a biography of Fitzgerald, *The Far Side of Paradise* (1951), and edited *Afternoon of an Author* (1958; a collection of writings by Fitzgerald) and *Scott Fitzgerald: A Collection of Essays* (1962). In this excerpt, Mizener discusses Fitzgerald's relation to history, and his representation of wealth and class in America.]

Scott Fitzgerald had an imaginative sense of the experience of the 1920s, was indeed a writer so closely related to his time and he was in danger of being wholly absorbed by his sense of it and of writing books that would not survive it. . . .

The meaningful question to ask of Fitzgerald's work is how much it reveals about the quality of his time, the movement of attitude and feeling in it; how much it penetrates to meaning and motive, that is, in the period, however statistically unrepresentative may be the specific particulars it selects from the period to convey this understanding. These things, too, are a kind of history, perhaps the essential kind of history, and of it Fitzgerald's sense was extremely acute. [. . .]

It was no doubt a dramatic and exciting time in America, the 1920s. . . . It was a period that ran its course rapidly and excitingly. Fitzgerald said afterwards that it lasted almost exactly ten years, beginning with the May Day riots of 1919 "when he police rode down the demobilized country boys gaping at the orators in Madison Square" and leaping, as he put it, "to a spectacular death in October 1929.

What it felt like to be living through the early days of that decade is most beautifully realized in one of the finest of Fitzgerald's early stories, "May Day." Of the so-called "May Day riots" described with such wonderful irony in that story, Fitzgerald said elsewhere that "we didn't remember anything about the Bill of Rights until Mencken began plugging it, but we did know that such tyranny belonged in the jittery little countries of south Europe. If goose-livered business men had this effect on the government, then maybe we had gone to war for J. P. Morgan's loans after all." [. . .]

We Americans seem to suffer under a peculiar taboo about wealth. By some kind of conspiracy of silence, we work together to persuade ourselves that we thing what we call "beautiful *homes*" . . . are nice enough but not necessary to our virtue and happiness. Almost pathetically, for a business civilization, we even cling to the pretense that wealth is not the foundation of social position. Fitzgerald's imagination was somehow freed from this taboo; he recognized clearly, and did not even know he was not supposed to say, that the rich are different from you and me—and luckier in the possibilities of their lives. Thus he was able to perceive without confusion all there was to know about the subtle and complex structure of sentiment and attitude we build up almost from birth around objects and activities that are conspicuously expensive. . . .

He was not strikingly optimistic about the prospect of our not being damned by our materialism, of our dream's surviving its entanglement with particularly expensive objects.

—Arthur Mizener, *F. Scott Fitzgerald* (New York: McGraw-Hill Book Company, 1973): pp. 99–100, 103, 110–111.

CHARLES E. SHAIN ON FITZGERALD AND OTHER WRITERS

[Charles E. Shain wrote a study, *F. Scott Fitzgerald*, in 1961. In this excerpt, he indicates some of the authors Fitzgerald may have been responding to in "May Day."]

"May Day" was probably a discarded beginning to a novel about New York. May Day 1919 was the exact day, Fitzgerald said later, when the Jazz Age began. The story is planned to carry more weight than the usual early Fitzgerald story. It uses three plots with intertwining action, like a Dos Passos chronicle novel, opens with an economic motif, the Manhattan crowds staring greedily at the glowing contents of shop windows, and in other ways gives evidence of Fitzgerald's willingness to steal some pages from the American naturalist. The mob scenes and the two "primitives," the foot-loose soldiers looking for whiskey, may have come not from Fitzgerald's observation but from the novels of Norris and Dreiser. But if these are the story's weak spots they are also marks of its ambition. Fitzgerald wanted to use the whole loud and anarchic world of Manhattan as the background of his own forlorn state in the spring of 1919 when he was an ex-lieutenant writing advertising copy, broke, and heartsick at the loss of his girl. The portrait he draws of Gordon Sterrett, in the midst of the big money, desperately poor and depending on alcohol, shows how intensely he could project fears for his own failures—and perhaps how fascinated he would always be with the drama of failure. "I can't stand being poor," Gordon says, "You seem sort of bankrupt—morally as well as financially," says his rich Yale classmate. "Don't they usually go together?" Gordon asks. At the big dance at Delmonico's Gordon gets drunk and tells a girl how it feels to go to pieces, "Things have been snapping inside of me for four months like little hooks on a dress, and it's about to come off when a few more hooks go." Metaphors of bankruptcy and of coming unhooked are going to turn up later when Fitzgerald contemplates his own sense of failure.

—Charles E. Shain, "F. Scott Fitzgerald," in *Pamphlets on American Writers* (Minneapolis: University of Minnesota Press, 1967): pp. 27–28.

SERGIO PEROSA ON UNITY IN "MAY DAY"

[Sergio Perosa, an Italian scholar, is the author of *The Art of F. Scott Fitzgerald* (1965) and *American Theories of the Novel* (1983). In this excerpt, he argues that "May Day" is a structured aesthetic whole, and that Fitzgerald's craft had developed since his first novel, *This Side of Paradise*.]

A deep moral sense and a budding social awareness, structurally united in an organic whole, went into the writing of the surprisingly successful "May Day." Just as [*This Side of Paradise*] proposed to be the history of a generation, this long story is intended to be the history of a period, "the general hysteria of that spring which inaugurated the Jazz Age (1919)." A series of apparently unrelated incidents is woven into a pattern and unified by the particular historical background in which they are set. The story opens with a quick sketch of the background and then introduces one after another the adventures of various characters. Gordon Sterrett, ruined by the war and by his weakness, is desperately trying to borrow some money that will save him; Philip Dean, enriched by the war, turns down his request for a loan; Edith, who had once been Gordon's girl, recoils from him, horrified at his degradation, when she meets him at a party. To the same party, after dragging through the city on a drunken spree, come Rose and Key, two poor soldiers, who end up in a closet from which, symbolically, they come out only to steal drinks, or to meet Peter Himmel, Edith's neglected escort. Gradually, the mood of the party changes from gaiety to hysteria. Edith goes to visit her brother who works for a socialist paper and is caught in the office when a mob of demonstrators give vent to their restlessness and rage. This new, frightening experience brings about a profound change in Edith. Her brother is wounded; one of the two soldiers is killed. Edith watches with horror as Philip and Peter continue their spree, going from one bar to another, while Gordon goes back to the vulgar Jewel and commits suicide. Begun with a documentary purpose, "May Day" becomes an artistic achievement because of its dramatic presentation of a series of events and its careful plot—the soul, as Aristotle said, of the action. It is, in fact, the masterful disposition of the various episodes and the way in which they are related and woven together that make the story interesting. There are no loose ends, no incongruous parts in the story, and each thread is taken up and given its final twist at the end with an economy of means that makes it possible for a vast frame of events to find its focus. Fitzgerald faced the structural problem of a skillful plot-disposition with full aesthetic awareness. For the first time he made use of the technique of foreshortening which Henry James had advocated and which he was later to develop with greater skill. There is a corresponding maturity in the perception of the theme. Fitzgerald often confused himself with his characters, but here he assumed an objective viewpoint that permitted him to combine a wide frame of reference with a particular relief given to each separate scene and to its thematic relevance. To give a picture of a particular historical moment, he did not avail himself of the reactions of a single character, but instead made up that picture by resorting to distinctly varied characters. This was a step forward from *This Side of Paradise.*

—Sergio Perosa, *The Art of F. Scott Fitzgerald* (Ann Arbor: University of Michigan Press, 1965): pp. 32–33.

ANTHONY J. MAZZELLA ON PARADOX IN "MAY DAY"

[In this excerpt, Anthony J. Mazzella explores the paradox inherent in the title, which provides, in turn, the story's primary aesthetic principle.]

The title, for example, is a paradox, specifying numerous opposites when related to the story. First, it denotes the day (May 1, 1919) when most of the random incidents occur—largely involving violence and death. Next, besides denoting the date of occurrence, the title has several suggestive connotations which, because they are both apt and capable of wide application, create a sense of life where the events in the story create an opposite effect: a sense of defeat, despair, the abyss. May Day, of course, commemorates the working class, but in the story we have confusion in the working class. There, the Socialists supporting the workers are attacked by the soldiers of that same working class. As Henry Bradin observes to his sister, "The human race has come a long way . . . but most of us are throw-backs; the soldiers don't know what they want, or what they hate, or what they like. They're used to acting in large bodies, and they seem to have to make demonstrations. So it happens to be against us. There've been riots all over the city to-night. It's May Day, you know." Thus, elements of the same class are working against each other; supposed allies become enemies, similarities become opposites, and the day of commemoration becomes the night of death and destruction. But May Day connotes more than a commemoration—in the story, a commemoration gone awry. It connotes the celebration of a spring festival, crowning a May Queen, dancing around a May pole, the advent of new life; but in the story we encounter the reverse: the dance around a May pole is a mob assault on a building, the crowning of a May Queen is Edith Bradin facing a retinue of attackers and consoling her brother whose leg has just been broken by the men he calls "'the fools,'" and the advent of new life is the death of Carrol Key and the suicide of Gordon Sterrett. Finally, "May Day," from the French *m'aidez,* means "help me"; it is the familiar distress call, what all the beleaguered characters in the story itself are crying out without ever expressing the words but which a kind of nameless chorus in the prologue does utter: "May Heaven help me." The title, therefore, names a day, signals an event, makes a plea. The title's amplitude, thus, in not only referring to the time of the story but also in giving connotations of commemoration, celebration, and help, offers a richness that counterbalances the defeatism of the plot and produces a tension of opposites which, as we shall see, is sustained throughout the work.

—Anthony J. Mazzella, "The Tension of Opposites in Fitzgerald's 'May Day,'" *Studies in Short Fiction* 14, no. 3 (Fall 1977): 380–381.

ROBERT K. MARTIN ON HOMOSEXUALITY IN "MAY DAY"

[Robert K. Martin has taught at Concordia University in Montreal, and writes on American literature. In this excerpt, he reads the relationship between Gordon Sterrett and Philip Dean as a literary representation of homoerotic desire.]

Fitzgerald's prologue to "May Day" suggests that one is to see the threads of the narrative as part of a single strand, or even to see that they are the same thread, viewed differently: "there were many adventures that happened in the great city, and, of these, several—or perhaps one—are here set down." But despite this invitation, critics have not been able to see the identity of theme—the crisis of the male-bonding relationship. Return from war, like graduation from college, was potentially frightening for Fitzgerald's characters, as they lost their sense of comradeship and found themselves suddenly alone.

In the first section of the story, Fitzgerald emphasizes carefully that the encounter is between two very attractive young men: Gordon is "small, slender, and darkly handsome . . . with unusually long eyelashes" and Philip is "blond, ruddy, and rugged under his thin pajamas." The scene is then eroticized. Philip goes off to take a shower as soon as Gordon arrives, then emerges from the bathroom, apparently nude, "polishing his body." He continues to display himself to Gordon, then "survey[s] his shining self complacently in the mirror" and finally, about half a page later, "drap[es] himself reluctantly in fresh underwear."

The erotic basis of their competitive relationship is clear. Philip is aware of his superiority, both financial and sexual, over Gordon. He uses his display of his body as an element of sadistic control, as assertion of power. Gordon, who has failed in his career and failed in his romantic life, undergoes a ritual enactment of Philip's superior virility. The theme becomes crucial to the story, as Gordon is increasingly tormented by his own sense of failure until he commits suicide. Fitzgerald used the erotic relationship between two men as a foundation for sexual humiliation, and he apparently recognized that the competition for a woman in the world of the fraternity dance is a rivalry acted out primarily between the two men, in sexual-political terms, with the woman remaining quite distant, at best the anticipated reward. The Gordon-Philip relationship hovers on the boundary of love and hatred. "For an instant before they turned to go their eyes met and in that instant each found something that made him lower his own glance quickly. For in that instance they quite suddenly and definitely hated each other."

—Robert K. Martin, "Sexual and Group Relationships in 'May Day': Fear and Longing," *Studies in Short Fiction* 15, no. 1 (Winter 1978): 99–100.

JAMES TUTTLETON ON SOCIALISM IN "MAY DAY"

[James Tuttleton is a professor of literature at New York University. He has written on Washington Irving and Henry James and is the author of *The Novel of Manners in America*

(1972). In this excerpt he discusses the story's representation of socialism.]

It is doubtless true that Fitzgerald was an individualist, hustling with the best of the entrepreneurs to make a dollar—in his case from fiction. And it is unarguable that his views were sketchy and based more on feeling than on dialectical materialism. But his socialist sympathies color his fiction and should not be lightly regarded by those who would grasp the ideological subtext of his work.

In "May Day," however, the treatment of socialism is a rather confused and ambivalent affair. On the one hand, we are made to sympathize with the Socialists as idealistic victims of the mindless mobs which rove the streets. The man on Sixth Avenue who is beaten up for haranguing the crowd on J. P. Morgan's and John D. Rockefeller's war beautifully adumbrates the fate of Henry Bradin, who is assaulted in his office by Rose, Key, and the mob. The mindless chant, "Kill the Bolsheviki—We're Americuns," is artfully satirized as the raving of those who have already been shown to be less than fully human.

Yet the Socialists presented here are not wholly noble political standard-bearers of the brotherhood of man. Something of Fitzgerald's own American nativism is suggested in the language describing the street-corner orator as a "gesticulating little Jew with long black whiskers"; the *Trumpet* office worker Bartholomew, described as giving "the impression of a Middle-Western farmer on a Sunday afternoon," is called "loosely fat." And before we ever meet him, Henry Bradin is described by Gordon Sterrett as "sort of a socialistic nut"; we later learn that he has left a Cornell instructorship in economics to come to New York in order, in Fitzgerald's words, "to pour the latest cures for incurable evils into the columns of a radical weekly newspaper." A member of the upper class, given to radical chic, Bradin is described as dissociated from the working class he presumes to help. Twice he is described as having "far-away eyes" that seem "always fixed just over the head of the person to whom he was talking," and when the soldiers break into the newspaper office and he declaims his propaganda with his "far-away eyes fixed over the heads of the crowd," it is no wonder that they break his leg. As a visionary idealist, he cannot establish any human connection with those for whom socialism was supposed to be the only panacea.

—James W. Tuttleton, "Seeing Slightly Red: Fitzgerald's 'May Day'" in *The Short Stories of F. Scott Fitzgerald*, ed. Jackson R. Bryer (Madison: University of Wisconsin Press, 1982): pp. 189–190. ☙

[Robert Roulston teaches at Murray State University in Kentucky and is the author of articles on Fitzgerald and coauthor (with Helen H. Roulston) of T*he Winding Road to West Egg: the Artistic Development of F. Scott Fitzgerald* (1995). In this excerpt from his essay "Fitzgerald's 'May Day': The Uses of Irresponsibility," he comments on the modernist aspect of the story's aesthetic design.]

"May Day" seems modern in a way that the *Post* stories and even *The Great Gatsby* and *Tender Is the Night* do not. Much of that avant-garde aura comes from the pacing of the story more than from the structure. In 1920—and indeed long afterwards—modernity meant angularity, jaggedness, disconnectedness. It meant the dissonance of Stravinsky, the distortions of Picasso, the fragmentation of Joyce and Eliot. In *This Side of Paradise* Fitzgerald made some gestures toward this type of sensibility by altering his narrative method from section to section much as Joyce had done in *A Portrait of the Artist as a Young Man* and would soon do on an even grander scale in *Ulysses*. [. . .]

A similar gesture pervades "May Day." The cynical asides, the mocking preface, and the fragmented narrative do not obliterate the conservatism that was always a part of Fitzgerald's character. Just as Gordon Sterrett and Edith Bradin look back nostalgically on their own prewar days, so Fitzgerald reaches back to traditional forms of fiction. The story is less an experiment in form than a speeded-up version of a nineteenth-century novel with multiple plots, chance encounters, theatrical climaxes, and tidy denouements. The effect, however, of forcing into a few pages what Dickens would have put in hundreds is that of a motion picture film run at high speed. All is jerky, ludicrous, and surreal. "May Day," then, becomes a frenzied film clip of the birth of the Jazz Age. Its disparate elements, juxtaposed so daringly, do not coalesce and should not, because underlying both the action and the language are two irreconcilable emotions—disgust and elan. Perhaps only a story that should not be taken altogether seriously could adequately capture simultaneously this incongruous pair of attitudes that, in their very incompatibility, seem to capture the *Zeitgeist* of the early 1920s. Fitzgerald, of course, was already becoming the self-proclaimed bard of that *Zeitgeist* and was well upon his way toward viewing himself as both its exemplar and its victim.

—Robert Roulston, "Fitzgerald's 'May Day': The Uses of Irresponsibility," *Modern Fiction Studies* 34, (Summer 1988): no. 3 p. 212.

ALICE HALL PETRY ON FAILED LOVE IN "MAY DAY"

[Alice Hall Petry, a professor of literature and women's studies at Rhode Island School of Design, has written on George Washington Cable, Kate Chopin, and Anne Tyler. She is the author of *Fitzgerald's Craft of Short Fiction: The Collected Stories, 1920–1935* (1989). In this excerpt, she argues that the primary theme of "May Day"—disillusionment—is most clearly articulated through Fitzgerald's representation of failed romantic love.]

There is no question that Gordon is having problems with the ladies. An avowed heterosexual, Gordon has been in love with Edith Bradin for years, and though Fitzgerald tells us little about their relationship beyond the fact that they dated while Gordon was at Yale, it is clear that they had felt strongly about each other. The subsequent cooling of their relationship seems to have been initiated by Gordon. Never having had any sort of showdown with upper-class Edith, Gordon has become involved with lower-class Jewel—a scaling-down of romantic expectations which reflects his own sense of being no longer worthy of Edith. Edith, however, still clings to the collegiate dream image of pre-disillusionment Gordon. "I'm made for love" she thinks as the dance at Delmonico's begins, and having rejected her date for accidentally mussing her hair, she finds herself conjuring up "another dance and another man, a man for whom her feelings had been little more than a sad-eyed, adolescent mooniness. Edith Bradin was falling in love with her *recollection* of Gordon Sterrett" (emphasis added). Fitzgerald makes it clear that what Edith had felt for Gordon was not mature love, but an infatuation with a dream. Her continued affection for him reflects a selective memory, an idea, rather than the reality, and she is jolted visibly when she sees the actual Gordon at the dance: "She had seen Gordon—Gordon very white and listless, leaning against the side of a doorway, smoking and looking into the ballroom. Edith could see that his face was thin and wan—that the hand he raised to his lips with a cigarette was trembling." The closer she comes to him, the more disillusioning he is. His eyes are "blood-streaked and rolling uncontrollably," He whines that he has become "a damn beggar, a leech on my friends," and he admits that he's "very gradually going loony": "As he talked she saw that he had changed utterly. He wasn't at all light and gay and careless—a great lethargy and discouragement had come over him." No wonder talking to him generates only "an unutterable horror," and she withdraws her hand when he tries to touch it. But unlike Gordon, the resilient Edith recovers from her disillusioning encounter with her former lover and immediately begins planning for her next affair: "—Love is fragile—she was thinking—but perhaps the pieces are saved, the things that hovered on lips, that might have been said. The new love words, the tendernesses learned, are treasured up for the next lover."

The case of Jewel Hudson is more problematical. Refusing to depict her as a girl of the streets with a heart of gold, Fitzgerald has her threaten to blackmail Gordon over their intimacies; but he also depicts her as apparently genuinely concerned over Gordon's well-being. Learning he has been ill, she announces, "I don't care about the money that bad. I didn't start bothering you about it at all until you began neglecting me," and she goes on to say, "I wanted to see *you*, Gordon, but you seem to prefer your somebody else." She seems like an essentially decent woman—yet Gordon will commit suicide when he realizes that he is "irrevocably married" to her. The problem, then, is not Jewel, but what marriage to her represents: it confirms that he can no longer maintain the dream of a relationship, now or ever, with the girl who symbolizes his pre-disillusionment life, Edith Bradin.

A relationship with a woman can, then, confirm either the attainment of a dream or its irrevocable loss.

—Alice Hall Petry, "Fitzgerald's Craft of Short Fiction: The Collected Stories 1920–1935," (Ann Arbor: UMI Research Press, 1989): pp. 68–69

Plot Summary of
"The Diamond as Big as the Ritz"

"The Diamond as Big as the Ritz" was first published in *The Smart Set* in June 1922 and was subsequently included in *Tales of the Jazz Age* (1922). It belongs to the same period as "May Day," although the two stories differ widely in subject matter and genre. "Diamond" has been called a fantasy, a romance, a tall tale, and a fairy tale. Its fantastic mood owes something to Hollywood and the emerging motion-picture industry, which so fascinated and exasperated Fitzgerald. He hoped to sell "Diamond" to the studios; he had done so successfully with several other short stories, including "Head and Shoulders" and "The Offshore Pirate." But the fantasy parodies Hollywood's tendency to exaggerate. The observational realism that characterizes much of Fitzgerald's writing is not wholly absent from "Diamond," but it is trained on a naive narrator's response to a fantastic and surreal environment. This dual approach gives the story its humor, its self-deflating irony.

John T. Unger, the story's protagonist, comes from "a family that had been well-known in Hades—a small town on the Mississippi River—for several generations." In this opening line of the story, Fitzgerald begins to create its humor. The name "Hades" provides a one-line gag that recurs throughout the story: all the schoolboys ask John, "Is it hot enough for you down there?" As a literary repetend, the "Hades" joke is cheap; it registers as slick comedy befitting a vaudeville routine or the popular magazines that printed Fitzgerald's stories. Although Fitzgerald uses this line to create a continuity through the story, he also mocks its fatuousness. After all, John is bored by the monotony of the jokes that his hometown's name evokes. The disingenuous tone reminds the reader that this is an artificial realm of facile entertainment, and so Fitzgerald plays down the illusion he sets out to create; he deflates his own fantasy and makes reading it as a serious allegory difficult.

Ironically, the slick magazine in which Fitzgerald intended the story to appear (*The Saturday Evening Post*) rejected it—it was too heady, too deep, too unusual. In fact, despite both its occasional slapstick humor and its fantastic setting, "Diamond" is usually considered a bitter allegory about wealth's power to corrupt. The Washington family has wealth that invites literary hyperbole—as the title proclaims: They are sitting on a diamond as big as the Ritz-Carlton Hotel. At first, their world seems like a paradise. John Unger believes he has entered a garden of Eden or found El Dorado. But all is not as it seems: the Washingtons are corrupt and embattled. Their plan to keep the diamond a secret supposedly stems from a paternalistic wish to protect the marketplace from instability, but it soon necessitates corruption and the use of force. John will be murdered to keep the secret safe, like a long list of guests before him. The smooth golf course may lack sand, but its trap is full of human captives.

The fact that airplanes pose the strongest threat to the Washingtons' fortune allegorically makes their reign conservative, Luddite, old-fashioned. The Washingtons may represent that extreme upper echelon of wealthy American capitalists (such as William Randolph Hearst, J. P. Morgan, and John D. Rockefeller) who have enough money to buy anything, who own the means of production, and who often may seem above the law. More specifically, the Washington compound resembles a Southern plantation. Its operations are based on an anachronistic and illegal economy: slavery. The Washingtons have kept their slaves ignorant of the Civil War's outcome; they have denied history. Fitzgerald stages the contest between the Washingtons and the outside world in terms of modernization and technology: because the Washingtons cannot control advanced machines like airplanes, the march of history will deprive them of their secret.

Fitzgerald's attitude toward the rich was complicated, which is made apparent in the story. Although in his notebooks Fitzgerald called himself a "Marxian," he was not a critic of capitalism. He did believe that money was one of the most important factors in life. His famous conviction that the rich are fundamentally "different" evoked exasperation from Hemingway, who undercut him in print by agreeing that the rich are different: they have more money.

In "Diamond," the concept of unlimited wealth obviously fires Fitzgerald's imagination. Like the "moving picture fella" who is "used to playing with an unlimited amount of money," Fitzgerald imagines the château on a grand scale. (The "moving picture fella" makes an ironic figure for the author, since he is illiterate.) Fitzgerald brings this fantasy world to life—but he also blows it to smithereens. As we have already seen, such a vast amount of wealth corrupts. Moreover, the story serves as a warning not to put all one's faith in riches, because even the largest fortunes can go bust.

The young lovers John and Kismine, along with Kismine's sister Jasmine, escape with their lives, but without even a small handful of diamonds. Fitzgerald marks their return to the "real" world by making them lose their fortune—the money was only a dream, a thing of which stories are made. As John predicts to Kismine, "you will grow old telling incredulous women that you got the wrong drawer" of jewels. A "diamond as big as the Ritz-Carlton Hotel" ultimately belongs to those who can tell about it, because it exists only in the realm of the imagination.

The young lovers get away without the fortune, and so Fitzgerald resolves a problem that recurs elsewhere in his fiction: the inability of the poor boy to woo the rich girl. Fitzgerald often makes money—or, more properly, the lack of it—an obstacle to romantic love. Gatsby cannot marry Daisy in *The Great Gatsby* because he does not have the means to support her until too late, after she has married someone else. This paradigm obsessed Fitzgerald, and he encountered it in life as well as fiction. Zelda Sayre did not marry him until he began to achieve success, and even as a younger man he had apparently lost a girlfriend over financial inequality. (Once while visiting Ginevra King, Fitzgerald is said to have overheard the remark that "poor boys shouldn't think of marrying rich girls." The point is not whether it actually happened, but that the anecdote is so well-known and often repeated.)

In "The Diamond as Big as the Ritz," this problem takes on the dreamlike proportions of life and death. Mr. Washington dreads the thought of Unger as a prospective son-in-law so much that he plans to kill him at the end of the summer. Even though the lovers escape, Fitzgerald deflates the romance of the story's ending. They lose their fortune, they may also lose their happiness, and they will certainly lose their youth. Near the end, John remarks, "Everybody's youth is a dream, a form of chemical madness." Fitzgerald indulges in this terrible bit of dialogue (coming from our supposedly naive and youthful narrator), and rends the fabric of the illusion woven by the story. John continues, "let us love for a while, for a year or so," expressing a view that is either jaded or realistic but is certainly out of keeping with fairy-tale endings. Instead of riding off into the sunset with his princess, John T. Unger wraps himself in a blanket and goes to sleep, preferring to return to a world of dreams.

Many critics have connected the dreamland of the story with the American dream: the hope that in America, anyone can achieve his or her aspirations. Fitzgerald may be satirizing the fact that all too often, people aspire to wealth rather than something more personally fulfilling. In particular, the crass materialism of Mr. Washington's appeal to God seems to be Fitzgerald's way of conveying a sense that the original, more spiritual meaning of the American dream has been corrupted by greed. ❀

List of Characters in
"The Diamond as Big as the Ritz"

John T. Unger, the story's protagonist, is a young man from Hades, a small town on the Mississippi. "The simple piety prevalent in Hades has the earnest worship of and respect for riches as the first article of its creed," and John's "radiant humility" before riches makes him the ideal naive narrator. His parents send John to St. Midas', "the most expensive and the most exclusive boys' preparatory school in the world," where he becomes the playmate of the super rich, and is invited to spend the summer "in the West" by a classmate, Percy Washington. Although young and impressionable, John occasionally utters callow truisms.

Percy Washington is heir to a fortune—as he declares to Unger, "My father is by far the richest man in the world." His extreme wealth comes at a price of a certain isolation: he is shy at school, and he brings his friend home even though he will have to be executed to protect the family secret. Once at the château, Percy appears happy in his luxurious surroundings, but the interest of the story veers away from him.

Colonel Fitz-Norman Culpepper Washington, already dead before the story opens, has amassed the largest fortune in the world. A direct descendant of George Washington and Lord Baltimore, he fought in the Civil War and then took his slaves west. There, he discovered the diamond, set about turning it into cash, and kept his slaves in bondage. He passed the fortune onto his only son.

Braddock Tarleton Washington, son of the Colonel and father to Percy, has managed to preserve the family secret against the latest threats of discovery—by airplane. About 40 years old, he has a proud, vacuous face, and he "smells of horses—the best horses." He rules with a combination of ruthlessness and cold humor, killing his houseguests and keeping his prisoners alive, perhaps as a sort of amusement. He proudly tries to bargain with God, promising material worship if only the family treasure can be kept. Rather than lose his fortune, he prefers to blow up the diamond, his château, and his family.

Kismine Washington, Percy's younger sister, is like the princess in the tower. She falls in love with the visitor, John Unger, and warns him of his danger. Despite her wealth, she is not sophisticated: "I never smoke, or drink, or read anything except poetry," she tells John. Her innocence contributes to the fairy-tale atmosphere of the valley. Like her brother, she shares her father's "chaste and consistent selfishness."

Jasmine Washington, Kismine's older sister, enjoys books about "poor girls who kept house for widowed fathers." She romanticizes poverty, living in a fantasy world that is the opposite of the world in "The Diamond as Big as the Ritz." She is a sentimental reader who indulges herself in heroic dreams of helping others by becoming a "canteen expert" in the First World War. At the end of the story, she offers to become a washerwoman and support her sister and John T. Unger.

Mrs. Washington is "aloof and reserved at all times." She loves her son, Percy, and seems mostly indifferent to her daughters. Drawing upon the tradition of the Gothic novel, Fitzgerald gives her an aura of mystery by making her Spanish. ❀

Critical Views on
"The Diamond as Big as the Ritz"

CHARLES WEIR, JR., ON FITZGERALD AND CLASS
IN AMERICA

[In this 1944 article, Charles Weir, Jr., discusses Fitzgerald's
understanding of class and wealth in American society.]

"The necessity to struggle," "the determination to 'succeed,'" "the old
dream of being an entire man"—here are the motifs of Fitzgerald's
work. And associated with them there is always wealth—"an opulent
American touch." Money drew him with a golden spell; there is in
American literature no more penetrating investigation of certain
aspects of its power. Not that Fitzgerald was ever very concerned
with how money was made. The analyses of a Dreiser, a Norris, or an
Upton Sinclair were not for him. Most of his characters have made
their million before they appear in his pages—in railroads, in mines,
in oil—it really does not matter. But there is no naïveté in this summary dismissal of origins. Fitzgerald was under no illusions as to the
means by which a fortune is generally acquired. His interest lay in
another direction: the fortune being made, what could be done with
it, what was done with it? Wealth meant power, magnificence; and it
was the only road to power. There are no old families in Fitzgerald.
None of his heroes traces his ancestry to the *Mayflower*. A few times,
chiefly in short stories, he tentatively explored the relationship
between Southern "first families" and Northern money, and the
South hardly wins even a moral victory. The very panoply and
ostentation of extreme wealth bewitched him: Dick Diver rides in
the motor car of the Shah of Persia, an extra-long, jewel-incrusted
vehicle with wheels and radiator of silver; when thirteen-year-old
Amory Blaine is stricken with appendicitis, Italy bound, four hours
out from land, the great ship wheels slowly and returns him to New
York. It was not life, Fitzgerald wrote, but it was magnificent. Some-
times his visions of riches passed beyond all reality and found
expression in fairy tales such as "The Diamond as Big as the Ritz."

—Charles Weir, Jr., "'An Invite with Gilded Edges': A Study of F. Scott
Fitzgerald," in *Virginia Quarterly Review* 20 (1944): pp. 140–141.

[Marius Bewley (1918–1973) was a prolific literary critic
and professor of American literature at Rutgers University.
His books include *The Eccentric Design* (1957) and *Masks
and Mirrors: Essays in Criticism* (1970). In this excerpt, he
analyzes Fitzgerald's description of Fish and argues that this
dreamlike story's major theme is a criticism of the American dream.]

Two paragraphs [in particular] are strangely impressive, not only
because they create the atmosphere of dream but because the twelve
men of Fish seem, in their shadowy way, to embody meanings that,
as in a dream, are both insistent and elusive. The Christian implications of the fish symbol are certainly intended by Fitzgerald, and
these are enforced by the twelve solitary men who are apostles
"beyond all religion." These grotesque and distorted Christian connotations are strengthened by their dreamlike relation to Hades on
the Mississippi where John was born. What we are given in these
paragraphs is a queerly restless and troubled sense of a religion that
is sick and expressing itself in disjointed images and associations, as
if it were delirious. The landscape imagery helps build up this
atmosphere. The religious imagery in these paragraphs is emphatic,
but it stands here for spiritual desiccation, for the absence of any
religion at all—even for the absence of the possibility of any religion.
'There was no altar, no priest, no sacrifice.' But even for the twelve
spiritually dead Americans of Fish, a persistent capacity for wonder
still survives, and the observation carries Dutch sailors who must
have held their breath in the presence of this continent, 'face to face
for the last time in history with something commensurate to their
capacity for wonder.' But no commensurate objects survive in the
American world, for the American dream could feed only on material, and therefore exhaustible, possibilities. It was, as Scott Fitzgerald
(a former Catholic who was never wholly at ease in his separation)
very well knew, incompatible with any form of Christianity. The
implicit contrast between the eternal promises of the old religion
and the material promises of the American dream that had so largely
taken the place of any orthodoxy in America provided the most dramatic and sinister note for Fitzgerald to strike as Percy and John

descended from the Transcontinental Express at the forlorn, symbolic village of Fish.

What we have to bear in mind is that this story is an attack on that American dream which critics have so often imagined Fitzgerald was engaged in celebrating throughout his writings. The fevered religious imagery of the passage I have quoted presents it, in the very beginning, as a kind of gaudy substitute for a sterile orthodoxy whose promises cannot compete with the infinite material possibilities that the dream seems to hold out to the faithful Americans. This initial religious note indicates how deeply Fitzgerald understood the American tradition of which he was so profoundly a part. But having sounded it once, he moves on through the rest of the story to analyze those material possibilities on the secular level at which Americans have believed Heaven to be attainable.

> —Marius Bewley, *The Eccentric Design* (New York: Columbia University Press, 1957).

RICHARD A. KOENIGSBERG ON LOSS OF INNOCENCE IN "THE DIAMOND AS BIG AS THE RITZ"

[In this excerpt from his article "F. Scott Fitzgerald: Literature and the Work of Mourning," Richard A. Koenigsberg argues that the end of the fantasy in the story is a literary representation of the individual's encounter with the reality principle and the loss of a narcissistic, childlike perspective.]

In "The Diamond as Big as the Ritz," the Washington Estate, an earthly paradise which survives in isolation in the hills of Montana, its existence known only to the Washington family and to the few who accidentally discover it, is the externalized form of the child's phantasy of the absolute joy and power of his infancy. It is a self-contained, narcissistic world, dominated by the pleasure principle, entirely free from the demands of reality. John Unger, spending his first year away from home, is brought to the Washington Estate by a schoolmate. Indeed, it is as if Fitzgerald is indicating that once cast from the maternal bosom, one immediately seeks to return to it, or at least, to locate its equivalent in the real world.

The story itself, however, after having detailed the nature of the miraculous Washington Estate, is concerned with its destruction, with its gradual confrontation with the external world and its capitulation to the forces of reality. In tracing the destruction of this ideal world, Fitzgerald is confronting the fact that once evicted from one's infantile paradise, one can never return to it. The phantasy of infantile omnipotence comes face to face with the fact of adult reality, and Fitzgerald concedes to the latter. For John Unger, however, the gradual destruction of the Washington Estate is concurrent with the development of his love for Kismine Washington. When the estate has been blown up, John, poignantly, and with a sense of having faced and survived the ultimate loss, says to Kismine, "Let us love for a while, for a year or so, you and me. That's a form of divine drunkenness we all can try." Having faced the destruction of his infantile phantasy world, John can, for the time being, turn toward external reality for a love-object.

In summary, "The Diamond as Big as the Ritz" represents Fitzgerald's confrontation with his fixation upon the narcissistic dreams of his childhood, and his effort, by destroying the externalized representation of these dreams, to come to terms with the impossibility of their gratification.

—Richard F. Koenigsberg, "F. Scott Fitzgerald: Literature and the Work of Mourning," *American Imago* 24 (1967): pp. 249–250.

ROBERT SKLAR ON FITZGERALD AND THE WESTERN TALL TALE

[Robert Sklar has taught American culture at the University of Michigan. His books include *F. Scott Fitzgerald: The Last Laocoön* (1967) and *Movie-Made America: A Cultural History of American Movies* (1975). In this excerpt, he explains that the story belongs to—and revises—the tradition of the Western tall tale.]

"The Diamond as Big as the Ritz" begins in the laconic, matter-of-fact tones that Van Wyck Brooks associated with the straight-faced Western humorists of the gilded Age. The style and the point of view of the novella are rendered so simply and conventionally that the satire on values arises not so much from exaggeration as from a bland openness. "'He must be very rich,' said John simply. 'I'm glad. I like very rich people. The richer a fella is, the better I like him.' There was a look of passionate frankness upon his dark face." As Brooks described the Western humorists, one of their most important qualities was their ability to please both frontier and genteel audiences by a complex interconnection of two sets of values. The frontiersmen laughed at themselves; genteel Eastern audiences laughed at the frontiersmen. However much his satire implied a criticism of genteel conventions, the Western humorist rarely took a position directly opposed to dominant Eastern values. The violence and fantasy exaggeration of his stories were aspects of the failure and impotence of frontier lawlessness and disorder. The importance of "The Diamond as Big as the Ritz," as it relates to this frontier tradition, is that it operates by the same style and form, but that its values are radically altered. The frontier setting and the conventions of the Western tall tale are retained, but they are used as grounds for satiric criticism of genteel Eastern values; the twelve pathetic men of Fish, the one element of actual frontier life in the story, are quickly passed over. The violence and fantasy exaggeration in "The Diamond as Big as the Ritz" are the aspects of success, and of the power of success, to create a lawlessness and disorder of its own; they are aspects of an apotheosis of success, the logical outcome of desires unexpectedly fulfilled. The two sets of values in complex interconnection—and in conflict—in "The Diamond as Big as the Ritz" are the American dream, and the American dream come true.

—Robert Sklar, *F. Scott Fitzgerald, The Last Laocoön* (New York: Oxford University Press, 1967): pp. 142–143.

Brian Way on Class Allegory in "The Diamond as Big as the Ritz"

[Brian Way is the author of *F. Scott Fitzgerald and the Art of Social Fiction* (1980). In this excerpt, he describes the class allegory in the story, and comments on Fitzgerald's role in the formation of a distinctively American literary tradition.]

In "The Diamond," he presents the historical evolution of a class. The money his young people spend so nonchalantly has its own story—the history of America in the Gilded Age. Fitzgerald traces it through his account of the Washington family's rise to fortune—a brilliant mingling of burlesque and melodrama.

It's a story of the West—Fitzgerald had recognized from the beginning that American wealth is a specifically Western phenomenon. Shortly after the Civil War, Culpepper Washington discovers and appropriates a diamond mountain in an unexplored corner of Montana. His exploit seems scarcely more fantastic than some of the actual episodes of lawless adventure and individual enterprise during this phase of the nation's westward expansion. Mining in many ways typifies the economic activity of the Gilded Age: ruthlessly and often wastefully exploitative, it is the ultimate expression of personal greed and of indifference to the idea of a civilization. . . .

Culpepper Washington represents the exploitative phase of American capitalism; his son Braddock belongs to the period of consolidation. He seals up the mine and concentrates his energies on safeguarding what he has. He is an expert in banking and investment, an evader of taxes, a corrupter of legislatures. In theory he dislikes violence, but in practice he finds himself compelled to maintain a private army and to murder those who threaten his security.

Fitzgerald sees the American rich not merely as heirs to an economic history, but as creators of a style. "The Ice Palace" offers a tentative sketch of what that style might be, but "The Diamond as Big as the Ritz" goes much farther in subtlety and range of suggestion. This is apparent in the description of Braddock Washington's château. . . .

The château is an expression of that "vast, vulgar, and meretricious beauty" which is perhaps the one distinctive style American civilization has evolved. Fitzgerald's actual writing in this description leaves a good deal to be desired. It takes itself too seriously: it lacks the comic and satiric note which is needed to bring out the latent absurdity in such a conception of the sublime and beautiful. When this passage is read in its context, however—in the light thrown upon it by other details of the story—it is seen to be subtler than one had at first supposed. When Percy Washington, for instance, explains to John that it was designed, not by an architect, a landscape gardener or a poet, but by a "moving-picture fella," everything becomes clear. The château is nothing more than a vast Hollywood set. Almost every detail of Fitzgerald's description calls attention to effects of lighting—he himself sees it as if he were a director or a cameraman. The figure of Mrs. Washington in the lighted doorway is not that of an aristocratic *grande dame*, but rather of a film star posed for a big scene. . . . The sense of the insubstantiality and impermanence which are inseparable from this equivocal kind of beauty is particularly apparent at the end of the story. The château and the diamond mountain itself disappear together in a blinding white flash and a black pall of smoke. So it is with the other expressions of the American style: the glitter and noise of the State Fair vanish overnight leaving only the empty prairie; the abandoned and unlighted movie-set lurks in a deserted canyon; the American city itself, seen through the eyes of Henry James's Europeans, is no more than a vast temporary encampment, an Arabian bazaar that might disappear without warning.

—Brian Way, *F. Scott Fitzgerald and the Art of Social Fiction* (London: Edward Arnold Publishers, 1980): pp. 68–69.

Lawrence Buell on the Representation of Time in "The Diamond as Big as the Ritz"

[Lawrence Buell teaches English Literature at Oberlin College. His books include *Design of Literature* (1973) and *Literary Transcendentalism* (1973). In this excerpt from his essay, "The Significance of Fantasy in Fitzgerald's Short Fiction," he discusses the representation of time in the story.]

The unreality of the Washington lifestyle is dramatized partly as a quixotic defiance of time. Braddock's empire was founded on the refusal to accept the consequences of the Civil War and maintained against increasingly greater odds as technology improved (geologic surveys, invention of aircraft). It is finally defeated by the rise of modern warfare. Just before his demise, Braddock, first seen as "about forty" and "robust," suddenly and fittingly ages into "a broken, white-haired man." This process starts during the scene where he tries to bribe God to turn back the clock, "calling to witness forgotten sacrifices, forgotten rituals, prayers obsolete before the birth of Christ." Through this ritual the symbolic implications of Braddock's character are momentarily given full extension, and he appears for an instant as an archetypal being who transcends all temporal limits. As "king and priest of the age of gold," he is not just the richest American entrepreneur, but a primal figure— "Prometheus Enriched," as the narrator somewhat enigmatically calls him. Even before he finishes praying, however, his dimensions begin to shrink, and the failure of his prayer implies either the obsolescence of his faith or the traditional idea that the gold-worshiper is bound to the wheel of fortune, which is a time-bound condition. When Braddock destroys himself, we seem to have returned to a world of comparatively normal time and probability. The château has virtually disappeared; John, Kismine, and Jasmine discover that they have no diamonds, only rhinestones; John tells us that his hometown isn't, after all, the prototypical Hades but just an ordinary place. All this is a bit like Alice waking up from her dream of wonderland.

Or from the dream of youth. "The stars," Kismine says,

> "make me feel that it was all a dream, all my youth."
> "It was a dream," said John quietly. "Everybody's youth is a dream, a form of chemical madness."

Like Braddock, John too has misunderstood or refused to accept the consequences of human time. Almost willfully failing to draw any connection between himself and the prisoners, John doesn't see how his summer must end. His absorption in his love affair with Kismine shows the same naive attempt to orient life around himself that the Washingtons have displayed in the creation of their estate. He admires—and imitates—the "chaste and consistent selfishness" of Kismine, Percy, and their father. Significantly, John's reintroduction to "real life" is almost as abrupt as Braddock's downfall. Realization of his plight, his escape, and the château's destruction all happen in less than a day. Almost the entire story consists of these events, plus events leading up to and including John's first day at the estate. There is no correspondence between chronological time and the proportions of the story. July passes in a hazy instant.

—Lawrence Buell, "The Significance of Fantasy in Fitzgerald's Short Fiction," in *The Short Stories of F. Scott Fitzgerald: New Approaches in Criticism*, ed. Jackson R. Bryer (Madison: University of Wisconsin Press, 1982): pp. 32–33.

MATTHEW J. BRUCCOLI ON THE HISTORY OF "THE DIAMOND AS BIG AS THE RITZ"

[Matthew J. Bruccoli has painstakingly collected and republished F. Scott Fitzgerald's oeuvre. In this excerpt from his biography of Fitzgerald, *Some Sort of Epic Grandeur* (1981), he discusses the themes and publication history of the story.]

During the fall Fitzgerald wrote three stories for ready cash: "Two for a Cent," "The Popular Girl" (a long story about St. Paul which the Post published in two parts), and "The Diamond as Big as the Ritz." The masterpiece, "Diamond," was declined by the high-paying magazines to which Ober offered it, even after Fitzgerald cut it from 20,000 words to 15,000. The story seemed baffling to some editors and blasphemous to others. Those who understood "Diamond" saw it as a satirical attack on the American success ethic or at least on the simple faith that equates wealth with virtue—a message that might offend the advertisers. Commercial magazines exist to sell advertising space, not to publish great fiction. Fitzgerald reported to Ober, "I am rather discouraged that a cheap story like *The Popular Girl* written in one week while the baby was being born brings $1500.00 + a genuinely imaginative thing into which I put three weeks real enthusiasm like *The Diamond in the Sky* [the original title] brings not a thing. But, by God + Lorimer, I'm going to make a fortune yet." The story went to *The Smart Set* for $300.

"The Diamond as Big as the Ritz," Fitzgerald's most brilliant fantasy, is much more than a supreme fairy tale. The diamond of the title is a diamond mountain in the West owned by the Washingtons, making them by far the richest family in the world. Nevertheless, the necessity of protecting the secret of the diamond interferes with the benefits of ownership. The Washington children routinely invite schoolmates for vacations, knowing that the visitors will be murdered. When the diamond is discovered by the authorities, Braddock Washington offers God a bribe before blowing it up. The story is susceptible to allegorical interpretations, but it is unlikely that Fitzgerald intended it as allegory. The meanings of "Diamond" are sufficiently clear. Absolute wealth corrupts absolutely and possesses its possessors.

—Matthew J. Bruccoli, *Some Sort of Epic Grandeur* (New York: Harcourt Brace Jovanovich, 1981): pp. 160–161.

ROBERT A. MARTIN ON HOLLYWOOD AND "THE DIAMOND AS BIG AS THE RITZ"

[Robert A. Martin is a professor of English at the University of Michigan. His work has appeared in *Modern Drama, Studies in American Fiction,* and *Michigan Quarterly Review.* In this excerpt, he discusses the representation of Hollywood and the film industry in the story.]

In "The Diamond as Big as the Ritz" (1922), published in *Tales of the Jazz Age,* Fitzgerald continued to play on the image of the movies at the creator of exterior extravagances by men who, like Joseph Bloeckman, had little personal vision, grace, or education. The Braddock Washington château, resting on a huge diamond in a Montana valley, was originally to have been designed by the joint efforts of "a landscape gardener, an architect, a designer of stage settings, and a French decadent poet left over from the last century," all of whom had been kidnapped by Washington and are representatives of the older, more traditional arts, encumbered by past conventions of style, form, and process. Though they had placed at their disposal any materials they might need and an unlimited work force, they were unable to come to any agreement, and all four "went mad early one morning after spending the night in a single room trying to agree upon the location of a fountain, and were now confined comfortably in an insane asylum at Westport, Connecticut."

If Fitzgerald is creating a fantasy with satiric overtones, it is of a highly unusual nature because of the implied criticism and perversely frank approach to the traditional arts (the East) versus the then new and untraditional film industry (the West). The traditional arts, having failed (gone mad), are unable to agree on a minor detail and are retired to an insane asylum in Connecticut. Undaunted, Washington engages the services of "the man we found who was used to playing with an unlimited amount of money, though he did tuck his napkin in his collar and couldn't read or write." Though "Diamond" has been praised for its imaginative sweep and implied criticism of the materialism that underlies the American Dream, it is in the criticism of the traditional arts as "impractical" that Fitzgerald makes an equally strong and most damning indictment. While "the moving-picture fella" is illiterate and ill-mannered, he is unencumbered by tradition and able to use money imaginatively—at least he manages to build the château where the others failed, and he quite possibly left the valley alive. And like his fellows in Hollywood, he was catering in a direct way to his audience. If that audience demanded a dream world removed from reality, he knew how to deliver it.

If Braddock Washington's private diamond mountain in Montana can be equated with easily and immediately available wealth in the West, Fitzgerald's private diamond mine was the movie industry, also in the West.

—Robert A. Martin, "Hollywood in Fitzgerald: After Paradise," *The Short Stories of F. Scott Fitzgerald: New Approaches in Criticism*, ed. Jackson R. Bryer (Madison: University of Wisconsin Press, 1982): pp. 132–133.

ROBERT ROULSTON AND HELEN H. ROULSTON ON FANTASY AND REALITY IN "THE DIAMOND AS BIG AS THE RITZ"

[Robert Roulston teaches at Murray State University in Kentucky and is the author of articles on Fitzgerald. He and

Helen H. Roulston are coauthors of *The Winding Road to West Egg: the Artistic Development of F. Scott Fitzgerald* (1995). In this excerpt, they compare the story's fantasy to the realism of Fitzgerald's other work.]

The story is one of Fitzgerald's most effective achievements. At its center is a grand idea. The execution of that idea is hardly less magnificent. The vision of the world's richest man ruling over a fairyland, where he can actualize his every whim, liberated Fitzgerald's imagination as few other ideas did. Freed of the need, in Hawthorne's words, to "aim at . . . fidelity, not merely to the possible, but to the probable and ordinary course of man's experience" demanded by realism, Fitzgerald could revel in a voluptuous contemplation of the boundless wealth that both obsessed and eluded him, being not merely beyond his grasp but beyond his ken as well. He could also, at least with his pen, smite its possessors, thus temporarily assuaging "the smouldering hatred" he later confessed to feeling toward the rich. Moreover, he could project onto the Washington family all his own hostility toward society at large, first, by making the Washington estate a microcosm of America and, then, by destroying that microcosm. At the same time he could indulge his yearning for glamour by depicting the Washingtons' milieu as more dazzling than any mere luxury hotel or mansion on Long Island. He could even appropriate snippets of literary exotica from writers great and small and make these borrowings his own much as the Washingtons possess whatever they choose to buy or steal.

But, however much it anticipates *Gatsby*, "The Diamond as Big as the Ritz" remains a detour in Fitzgerald's career. The writer who contrived the mythic town of Fish and the fabulous estate of Braddock Tarleton Washington might have devoted his subsequent career to fashioning Gothic fiction in the vein of Hawthorne or Poe. Perhaps he could have followed his youthful idol, H. G. Wells, into a didactic never-never land of science fiction. Yet nearly everything about "The Diamond as Big as the Ritz" suggests that, had he devoted most of his efforts thereafter to fantasy, the losses would have outweighed the gains. Gothic and science fiction writers abound. Fitzgerald alone had a sufficient grasp of both the surface and the underlying strata of the 1920s to eternalize its ephemera as he did in *Gatsby* and in numerous short stories. The imagined diamond as big as the Ritz-Carlton Hotel provided him with a valuable excursion. Ultimately, though, he had more to say about the Ritz itself—and about its rival, the Plaza, where he would soon write "Winter Dreams" and where Jay Gatsby would lose Daisy Buchanan and win greater fame than perhaps even his creator dared to imagine.

—Robert and Helen H. Roulston, *The Winding Road to West Egg: The Artistic Development of F. Scott Fitzgerald* (Cranbury, N.J.: Associated University Presses, 1995): pp. 113–114.

Plot Summary of
"Babylon Revisited"

"Babylon Revisited" first appeared in *The Saturday Evening Post* in February 1931 and was later collected in *Taps at Reveille* in 1935. To many, it is Fitzgerald's finest short story. He is above all a poet of nostalgia, elegiacally evoking the transitory nature of experience. His best writing makes us feel the desire to return to the past while reminding us of the impossibility of that return. In stories like "The Diamond as Big as the Ritz," the loss of youth and of dreams seems artificial and disingenuous, but in "Babylon Revisited," Charlie Wales's tragic relation to the past deserves the gravity Fitzgerald gives it.

The story opens with Charlie Wales in the Ritz bar, in Paris, which he finds empty and lonely. Old friends are gone away, and nothing is the same. Like the narrator of Proust's *Remembrance of Things Past*, Charlie seeks to understand the essence of what he has lost by invoking its physical presence. But "Babylon" is a state of mind and not an actual place, and Charlie cannot recapture its ethos merely by returning to the sites of his former life.

As the story unfolds, Fitzgerald complicates the theme of desire for the past by putting the past in conflict with the present. In fact, despite his inquiry at the bar, Charlie is not in Paris to remember or to seek out old friends; he is there to pursue a goal for the present and future: regaining his daughter Honoria. The Ritz bar conjures up a time of error and recklessness that ruined Charlie's health, sent his wife to her grave, and deprived him of his daughter's company. Haunting his old walks through Paris later that evening, Charlie has an epiphany: "he suddenly [realizes] the meaning of the word 'dissipate'—to dissipate into thin air; to make nothing out of something." The ravages of "vice and waste" resemble the passage of time, but are less inevitable and more regrettable. Charlie and his fellow revelers paid "for the privilege of slower and slower motion"—for losing track of time, which has taken a toll on the future.

In the struggle to regain custody of his daughter, Charlie's opponent is his sister-in-law, Marion Peters. Marion refuses to forgive and forget Charlie's mistakes. She cannot bring herself to believe that Charlie has changed. She finds sinister meanings in Charlie's remarks, misconstrues his visit to the Ritz bar that day, and bitterly echoes his protest that Helen, his wife, had died of "heart trouble," as if "the phrase had another meaning for her." Charlie insists that he can control himself and his problem with alcohol, but Marion remains mostly unconvinced. She claims to represent the memory of her lost sister, Helen. It seems that damage has been done somewhere in her past, as well. Her husband speaks with a certain familiarity about the dangers of "working her up" to a state in which she might "go to pieces." For Marion, holding herself together means holding onto the past—even its bitterness.

Just when Marion seems to be relenting, Fitzgerald creates a tragic intrusion. Two old acquaintances of Charlie's, Lorraine Quarrles and Duncan Schaeffer, who still inhabit the Babylon he left behind, interrupt his negotiations for his daughter. When they barge into the Peterses', they are blind to the tension they create. "They [are] gay, they [are] hilarious, they [are] roaring with laughter." By juxtaposing those happy terms with their disastrous effects on the Peters's domestic circle, Fitzgerald dramatizes the oblivion that alcohol induces. They bring the spirit of dissipation into the Peters home, turning the "something" of Charlie's request for his daughter to "nothing." To Marion, they pose a threat so great that she breaks down and turns her back on Charlie's rightful request for Honoria. Charlie finds himself isolated between the drunken inconsideration of his friends on the one hand and the defensive insularity of the Peterses on the other. Not only can he never recover his wife, he cannot recover his daughter. This punishment exceeds his crimes. "He was absolutely sure Helen wouldn't have wanted him to be so alone."

As the scholar Seymour L. Gross points out, Charlie's loss is Honoria's as well. She provides the story with its pathos, for although the reader can identify with both the injustice of Charlie's situation and his remorse, Honoria is wholly innocent in her loss. She wants the simple pleasure of living with her own parent, the person whom she loves "better than anybody" and who will love her in return. If Marion Peters is living her life entrenched in the past, and Charlie Wales is trying to live for the present, Honoria seems to be speeding into the future. "She was already an individual with a code of her own, and Charlie was more and more absorbed by the desire of putting a little of himself into her before she crystallized utterly. It was hopeless to try to know her in so short a time." Because youth flies by, the postponement of the father-daughter relationship seems tantamount to its loss.

The story ends back at the bar, and Fitzgerald has inverted what initially promised to be a search for the past. He dramatizes the truth of what Nick Carraway tells Gatsby in *The Great Gatsby:* you can revisit, but "you can't repeat the past."

Like Charlie Wales, the Fitzgerald of "Babylon Revisited" is an older, more mature, chastened writer than the Fitzgerald of former days, when he wrote "May Day" and "The Diamond as Big as the Ritz." He had experienced some losses not unlike the ones sketched in the story. His wife, Zelda Sayre Fitzgerald, had suffered nervous breakdowns, and his daughter, Scottie, had to be cared for by relatives. His drinking led to the "dissipation" of friendships and of the amount of time he could devote to writing, both of which he regretted. Nevertheless, Fitzgerald's style had evolved and his craft had improved. "Babylon Revisited" has an evenness and depth of tone that eluded him in his earlier stories. The work of his friend and fellow writer Ernest Hemingway may have honed Fitzgerald's craft and inspired him to economize. The initial meeting between Charlie and his daughter conveys feeling with a minimum of commentary:

> As he rang his brother-in-law's bell in the Rue Palatine, the wrinkle deepened till it pulled down his brows; he felt a cramping sensation in his belly. From behind the maid who opened the door darted a lovely little girl of nine who shrieked "Daddy!" and flew up, struggling like a fish, into his arms. She pulled his head around by one ear and set her cheek against his.
> "My old pie," he said.
> "Oh, daddy, daddy, daddy, daddy, dads, dads, dads!"

This initial meeting at the door is reversed when Lorraine and Dunc also struggle past the maid, to destroy the father-daughter reunion described in the passage above. "Babylon Revisited" is structured with many repetitions of images and locales, evoking the theme of revisitation—that desire to repeat the past. The use of internal echoes and thematic couplets represent, in literary terms, Fitzgerald's themes of revision, revisitation, and return. ❀

List of Characters in
"Babylon Revisited"

Charlie Wales, the protagonist, is "thirty-five and good to look at." He is trying to rebuild a life damaged by his abuse of alcohol. Lonely and haunted after losing his wife, he wants to regain custody of his daughter. A self-professed, hard-working man of business, he lost control when the 1920s boom gave him more than he could handle; by the end of it, "everything was gone." Having rationed himself to a single daily drink, he has regained an equanimity that balances the remorse and wistfulness he feels. He holds this sense of balance dear, vowing to love even his daughter with responsible restraint. Although he tries to fix his mind on the present ("The present was the thing—work to do and someone to love," he admonishes himself), the past exercises an inexorable power over him.

Honoria Wales, Charlie's daughter, is a serious and self-possessed girl of nine. She realizes that a custodial contest is taking place, and wants to be with her father. She is "already an individual with a code of her own," and Charlie wants to put "a little of himself into her before she crystallized utterly."

Marion Peters, Charlie's sister-in-law, cannot forgive Charlie for his past. She bitterly blames him for her sister's death. "A tall woman with worried eyes," she no longer possesses the "fresh American loveliness" that was hers in youth. Nervousness and perhaps something more have made her fragile and emotional on the one hand and unrelenting on the other. Despite her warm and "comfortably American" home, Marion is an unsympathetic character. Ironically, her inability to believe that Charlie has changed makes him "for the first time in a year" want a drink. Charlie's fear that Marion will poison his daughter's love for him may be justified, which adds to the pathos of his defeat.

Lincoln Peters's dispassionate caution makes him a foil to both his wife's overwrought emotions and to Charlie's intrepidness. He does not take financial risks and has never exposed himself to the excessive successes and failures that Charlie has experienced. He meets his responsibilities modestly. Although he feels a masculine camaraderie with Charlie and recognizes the latter's paternal claim to Honoria, his first responsibility remains with his wife.

Duncan Schaeffer, unlike Charlie, is still living a wild, inebriated life. For him, Paris remains Babylon. Although he is an old college friend of Charlie's, he functions primarily as a plot device, a walking reminder of Charlie's past that refuses to disappear and keeps turning up in unwanted contexts.

Lorraine Quarrles, Duncan Schaeffer's drinking companion, "a lovely, pale blonde of thirty," also reminds Charlie of his past. Her interest in Charlie is apparently flirtatious. When she reminds him of their nocturnal escapade through Paris on a tricycle, Charlie remembers that his wife had been jealous of Lorraine, though she said nothing. From Charlie's sober point of view, Lorraine cuts an almost pathetic figure, slurring her words and making herself too available. She inspires an almost visceral dislike in Marion Peters, and so acts as the literary catalyst that ultimately deprives Charlie of Honoria. ❀

Critical Views on
"Babylon Revisited"

SEYMOUR L. GROSS ON THE QUESTION OF REFORM IN "BABYLON REVISITED"

[Seymour Lee Gross has taught literature at the University of Detroit and at the University of Notre Dame. He is the author of *Images of the Negro in American Literature* (1966). In this excerpt, he analyzes the literary representation of Charlie Wales's reform.]

The action of "Babylon Revisited" begins and ends in the Ritz bar. This structural maneuver is absolutely right, for the bar is one of the story's chief symbols of the relentless impingement of the past on the present, though it is not until the end of the story after Charlie's defeat, that it clearly takes on this signification. Indeed, ironically enough, Charlie's initial appearance at the Ritz seems to imply precisely the opposite: the apparent separation of the past from the concerns, needs, and desires of the present. The very fact that Charlie can return to the hub of a life which had cost him his wife and his child does not at all indicate, as the story's most recent commentator has it, that the old way of life "still appeals to him" but rather demonstrates the extent and depth of his self-mastery and the confidence he feels in his belief that his wildly squandered yesterdays are over and done with, that there is no tab left for him to have to pick up.

The opening scene's primary function is to show how divorced Charlie feels from the blurred life of several years ago. His questions to the bartender about cronies from the past are mechanically curious but fundamentally uninterested. The news that "Mr. Campbell [is] a pretty sick man" and that Claude Fessenden cheated the bar of thirty thousand francs and is now "all bloated up" evokes no comment. The pricks to memory of "familiar names from the long list of a year and a half ago" strike no responsive chord. Charlie feels out of place and "polite" in the bar that, in the time of wine and roses, he had felt he had "owned." "It had gone back into France," he thinks. When he goes through the remembered ritual of placing his foot firmly on the bar rail and turning to survey the room, only a single pair of indifferent eyes "fluttered up from a newspaper in the corner." Charlie's dissociation from his past is capped by the brief bit of dialogue with which the scene ends:

> "Here for long, Mr. Wales?"
> "I'm here for four or five days to see my little girl."
> "Oh-h! You have a little girl?"

In the Babylon who "saith in her heart [I] shall see no sorrow," there can be neither children nor the risk of their loss. The figures there float rootlessly free of human ties and responsibilities, having sprung full-born from their skyrocketing blue chips and capacity for dissipation. The adults are the only children. "We *did* have such good times that crazy spring [Lorraine wistfully recalls in the letter to Charlie], like the night you and I stole the butcher's tricycle, and the time we tried to call on the president and you had the old derby rim and the wire cane." But Charlie Wales's return to Paris is an attempted return to fatherhood, an attempt to lay the ghost of his past childishness through the recovery of his lost child, Honoria. "Oh-h! You have a little girl?" is a bitterly reasonable question for one whose life had been nothing more than a "catering to vice and waste . . . on an utterly childish scale." After all, children have no children.

The tragedy is that Charlie no longer deserves such a question. There is in us a desire to find the present Charlie somehow deserving of his wretched fate—which is what perhaps accounts for Professor Harrison's reading—for it is easier to live with a belief in reasonable justice. But Fitzgerald does not allow us this luxury. Throughout the story he ironically stresses the splendid achievement of Charlie's reform. His sensitivity, poised intelligence, and quiet power over himself should be enough to get his daughter back. That moral renovation may not be enough is the injustice that lies at the center of the story.

—Seymour L. Gross, "Fitzgerald's 'Babylon Revisited,'" *College English* 25, no. 11 (November 1963): pp. 129–130.

THOMAS F. STALEY ON TIME IN "BABYLON REVISITED"

[Thomas Staley teaches at the University of Tulsa. He has written and edited numerous volumes on modern literature, including *Essays on the Modern Novel* (1968) and *Approaches to Joyce's Portrait: Ten Essays* (1970). In this excerpt, he explores the story's representation of time.]

The very title of the story suggests the movements of time and space. The scene is set in the modern city along the Seine, but we are intended to recall the ancient city on the banks of the Euphrates. Charlie Wales returns to Paris in order to claim his daughter and thus give meaning and purpose to his life. But just as Charlie has changed in the three years since he left Paris, so, too, has the world he left. In the opening scene in the Ritz bar he inquires about his former friends, but finds they have scattered, to Switzerland, to America. He notices a group of "strident queens" in the corner and is depressed because he realizes that "they go on forever" and are not affected by time.

Throughout Part I of the story Charlie is continually trying to turn back the clock. During dinner at the Peters' he looks across at Honoria and feels that "he wanted to jump back a whole generation." As he wanders the streets of Paris, Charlie Wales's attitude toward time is that of something lost. Throughout Part I all references to time are to the past; the hope for the future remains in the background.

There is a shift of emphasis in time as Part II opens. Charlie wants to forget the horrors of the past as he has lunch with Honoria. He deliberately chooses a restaurant that is "not reminiscent of champagne dinners and long luncheons that began at two and ended in a blurred vague twilight." Today is to be a special day; today is to be isolated into the present; but this is impossible, for out of that twilight world of the past "sudden ghosts" emerge. Two of the people who helped him to "make months into days" confront him in the restaurant, and the past impinges on the present, and also foreshadows its impingement on the future.

In this scene present, past and future fuse. Both past and future collide as Honoria, a symbol of the future, meets Lorraine and Duncan, symbols of the lurking past. This scene in which the past and future meet in the present also foreshadows the climax of the story in Part IV, when Lorraine and Duncan invade the Peters' home and in so doing both symbolically and literally destroy the future....

The final irony of Charlie's life is brought out in the final section of the story, part V, which is set again in the Ritz bar where the story opened. Paul, the bartender, points out the irony unknowingly when he says, "It's a great change." Charlie's' mind goes back to the past again, but now he sees himself in the eternal present, alone. He thinks back to a fixed period of time, the Wall street crash, and then to the time just before that when the snow wasn't real snow. "If you didn't want it to be snow, you just paid some money." To escape from the past Charlie tried to make a life for himself and Honoria, but now he must be concerned with only the hollow thought of buying her something. As the story ends, he must escape time and reality and dream again of Helen, who he is sure "wouldn't have wanted him to be so alone." Time and its ravages have left Charlie suspended in time with a nightmare for a past, an empty whiskey glass for a present, and a future full of loneliness.

—Thomas F. Staley, "Time and Structure in Fitzgerald's 'Babylon Revisited,'" *Modern Fiction Studies* 10, no. 1 (Winter 1964): pp. 386–388.

ROY R. MALE ON THE RETURN OF THE EXILE IN "BABYLON REVISITED"

[Roy R. Male has taught at the University of Texas and the University of Oklahoma. He is the author of *Hawthorne's Tragic Vision* (1957) and coeditor of *American Literary Masters* (1974). In this excerpt, he explores the theme of the returning exile in the story.]

What kind of story is "Babylon Revisited"? to this deliberately broad and blunt question the answers, whether from students, English teachers, or writers, would be something short of unanimous. Here are some typical student replies: "it's a good story."

"Babylon Revisited" belongs with a number of stories in which the protagonist returns after a prolonged absence, either to his home or to some substitute for it. This category we may call the story of the Exile's Return, and in American fiction it would include (among others) Washington Irving's "Rip Van Winkle," Nathaniel Hawthorne's "Ethan Brand," Hamlin Garland's "The Return of a Private," Henry James's "The Jolly Corner," Ernest Hemingway's "Soldier's Home," Theodore Dreiser's "The Old Neighborhood," Lionel Trilling's *The Middle of the Journey*, and Frederick Buechner's "The Tiger." Behind these American Stories, of course, are such prototypes as Ulysses returning to Penelope, Plato's myth of the cave, the Biblical account of the return of the prodigal son, and Dante's return from his vision of hell, purgatory, and paradise.

Certain themes are inherent in the basic situation of the man returning after a long absence. In fiction as in life, the most obvious and the most poignant is the mutability theme or, more specifically the sense of permanence and change. Although some aspects of the setting seem unchanged, their apparent permanence simply emphasizes the fundamental law of life, that all things pass. Thus we have in these stories something like the ubi sunt formula in poetry. Rip Van Winkle asks, "Where's Nicholas Vedder? Where's Brom Dutcher? Where's Van Bummel, the schoolmaster?" Gone, all of them gone. Even Vedder's wooden tombstone, Rip learns, is "rotten and gone." This, of course, is where Fitzgerald's story begins. "Where's Mr. Campbell?" "And George Hardt?" "And where is the Snow Bird?" "What's become of Claude Fessenden?" All gone, some of them "rotten and gone." In the Babylonian Ritz bar only the "strident queens" remain; "they go on forever."

The hero may ask about the men, his former friends, but the essential motivation for his return is always a reunion with some form of the feminine principle. She may be a person: the faithful wife as in "The Return of a Private," the daughter as in "Rip Van Winkle" and "Babylon Revisited," the stable and intimate friend Alice Staverton in "The Jolly Corner." Or it may be more abstract and symbolic: the "mother earth" invoked and then rejected by Ethan Brand, the "girls" that bother Krebs in "Soldier's Home," or the alma mater as in "The Tiger." Thomas Wolfe, whose fiction flowed forth from the archetypal patter of departure and return, described the impulse this way: "By the 'earth again' I mean simply the everlasting earth, a home, a place for the heart to come to, and earthly mortal love, the love of a woman, who, it seems to me, belongs to the earth and is a force opposed to that other great force that makes men wander, that makes them search, that makes them lonely, and that makes them both hate and love their loneliness."

As anyone who has returned home after a long absence will testify, the experience often has a dreamlike quality, a curious mixture of pain and pleasure as one feels his identity dissolving into two selves, past and present, private and public.

This theme of split identity recurs, as we shall see in "Babylon Revisited," where the basic question about Charlie is whether he is indeed "the old Wales," as his former friends call him, or the new.

A final theme given in the situation of the returning exile is that of freedom and responsibility. The mere fact that he has been gone suggests the possibility of egotism and escapism.

—Roy R. Male, "'Babylon Revisited': A Story of the Exile's Return," *Studies in Short Fiction* 2 (Spring 1965): pp. 270–277.

JOHN A. HIGGINS ON FITZGERALD AND AESTHETIC ECONOMY

[John A. Higgins has taught literature at the City University of New York and is the author of *F. Scott Fitzgerald: A Study of the Stories* (1971). In this excerpt, he praises and analyzes Fitzgerald's aesthetic economy in the story.]

What earns for "Babylon Revisited" the accolade of being Fitzgerald's finest story is, besides its thematic depth, simply that he does everything right. Fitzgerald showed frequently in previous stories that he could perform the technical feats required for superlative fictional art, but he was never able to avoid, in a story of magnitude, at least one considerable flaw until "Babylon Revisited." Here, aesthetic distance and point of view are tightly controlled. Charlie is the central intelligence, yet Fitzgerald refrains from his usual authorial interpretations: Charlie's thoughts are related without comment, even at the end. This effects just the right aesthetic distance, a balance of sympathy and detachment. The story's tone is carefully muted, from the description of the nearly deserted bar to that of "the fire-red, gas-blue, ghost-green signs [that] shone smokily through the tranquil rain" (the passage is used in *Tender Is the Night*). Fitzgerald's tendency to rhetoricize in the final passage is likewise restrained. The pervasively melancholy atmosphere of Paris forebodes Charlie's disaster. These foreshadowings lend an air of inevitability to the story which is only slightly marred by the fortuitous appearance of Lorraine and Duncan.

Although the story is long, it achieves economy by several means. By eliminating the usual large number of minor characters Fitzgerald not only achieves sharper character focus but also intensifies the impression of emptiness in the city. Also, he concentrates on a single incident rather than including scenes of the Waleses' married life, thereby not only achieving narrative economy but also avoiding a possible split in character focus and point of view.

The plot is constructed around a series of seven scenes set alternately without and within Marion's home. Thus Fitzgerald has set up for Charlie a continual reciprocating movement between his old and his new worlds, with the transitional passages, as Charlie travels between these worlds, supplying the atmospheric background of Paris. Scenes one and seven, the framing scenes, occur in the Ritz bar. Scenes two, four and six take place in Marion's home and depict Charlie's passage from hope to elation to defeat. The intermediate scenes, three and five, are similar to each other in structure, each with two parts: the first a hopeful, future-oriented conversation in a restaurant between Charlie and a character sympathetic to him, the second an intrusion of Duncan and Lorraine to remind him of the past and dampen his hope. Since scenes two, four and six deal with the present reality, it can be seen that Fitzgerald has interwoven another set of movements into the story: an in-and-out movement among past, present, and future. There is still a third pattern of movement, that of Charlie's emotional alternations between optimism and pessimism, hope and disillusion. The story's skewed triangular structure (the ascending leg covering about two-thirds of the story) reaches its apex in the fourth scene, the longest and most tense, where Marion's resistance to Charlie finally cracks. A second climax occurs in scene six, where all the forces and all the principal characters converge as the ghosts of Charlie's past burst in upon his present to destroy his future.

Fitzgerald's most consistent weakness, as this study has repeatedly shown, has been his inability successfully to end stories he has successfully begun. In "Babylon Revisited" he overcomes this greatest weakness as he overcomes all his others. There is no break in tone, structure, aesthetic distance or plausibility; if anything, the story becomes stronger toward its end. It becomes, then, Fitzgerald's finest achievement in the genre because all the technical qualities mentioned blend smoothly with a mature central theme which in turn is set against a historical background and a symbolic substructure that reflect and intensify that theme. Finally, it possesses inevitability; Charlie is caught in an "inescapable tragic knot."

—John A Higgins, *F. Scott Fitzgerald: A Study of the Stories* (New York: St John's University Press, 1971): pp. 123–124.

David Toor on Guilt in "Babylon Revisited"

[David Toor, in his article "Guilt and Retribution in 'Babylon Revisited'" (1974), suggests that narrative instability in the story reflects the psychological theme of guilt.]

Charlie Wales is not torn between the poles of two opposing worlds so much as he is torn by his own inner sense of guilt and his inability to expiate it. He is not morally renovated, only sicker and less able to cope with the guilt. In one part of him he wants his Honoria (honor) back, but in the deeper man, the guilt-ridden one, he knows he doesn't deserve her. He has exiled himself to a dream world free of past responsibilities—Prague—where he creates the fresh image of himself as a successful businessman. Of course the image cannot hold, and his distorted view of the real world leads him into delusion and jealousy: "He wondered if he couldn't do something to get Lincoln out of his rut at the bank." What kind of rut is Lincoln really in? A warm homelife that Charlie envies, children who love him, a neurotic wife, yes, but a reasonable contentment.

There are many hints through the story which point to these conclusions, and one of the most significant may be viewed as flaws in the technique of the tale. Fitzgerald chose a third-person limited point of view to tell the story, and the lapses, few as they are, are telling. All of the lapses—shifts from limited to omniscient—are concerned with the Peters. The three most important ones directly involve Marion:

> She had built up all her fear of life into one wall and faced it toward him.

> Marion shuddered suddenly; part of her saw that Charlie's feet were planted on the earth now, and her own maternal feeling recognized the naturalness of his desire; but she had lived for a long time with prejudice—a prejudice founded on a curious disbelief in her sister's happiness, and which, in the shock of one terrible night, had turned to hatred for him. It had all happened at a point in her life where the discouragement of ill health and adverse circumstances made it necessary for her to believe in tangible villainy and a tangible villain.

> Then, in the flatness that followed her outburst, she saw him plainly and she knew he had somehow arrived at control over the situation. Glancing at her husband, she found no help from him, and as abruptly as if it were a matter of no importance, she threw up the sponge.

In a way these passages are indeed flaws. Certainly a craftsman like Henry James, whose meanings so much depend on careful control of point of view, would not have allowed them to pass. . . . There is the possibility that these few passages can be read as consistent with a limited third-person point of view and that these were indeed Charlie's reactions to the situation.

But what these flaws may represent is Charlie's attempt to somehow put himself in a position to account for the (subconscious) terrors that were plaguing him on his return to Babylon. All three of these cited passages are explanations of the sources of Marion's hostility and her resignation in the face of Charlie's apparent renovation. Charlie is convinced that Marion has seen that he is a changed man. But it becomes more and more clear as we examine the story that he himself was by no means convinced.

Aside from the early action of leaving the Peters' address for Duncan Schaeffer at the bar—and Charlie's subsequent denial of any knowledge of how Duncan could have found it out—we need to examine in some detail what Charlie does and says throughout the story to understand just how completely he is caught between the psychologically necessary self-delusion that he is somehow blameless and changed, and the deeper recognition of his own guilt.

—David Toor, "Guilt and Retribution in 'Babylon Revisited,'" *Fitzgerald/Hemingway Annual 1973*, ed. Matthew J. Bruccoli and C. E. Frazer Clark, Jr. (Washington, D.C.: Indian Head Inc., 1974): pp. 156–157.

CARLOS BAKER ON TWO MOTIFS IN "BABYLON REVISITED"

[Carlos Baker (1909–1987) taught at Princeton University. He wrote and edited many books, including *Hemingway: The Writer as Artist* and *Ernest Hemingway: A Life Story*. In this excerpt from his article "When the Story Ends: 'Babylon Revisited,'" he identifies the two major motifs in the story, and explores their juxtaposition.]

Two motifs stand opposed in the story. One is that of Babylon, ancient center of luxury and wickedness in the writings of the Fathers of the Church. The other is that of the quiet and decent home life that Wales wishes to establish for his child. He defines the Babylon motif as a "catering to vice and waste." It is what used to happen every afternoon in the Ritz bar when expatriated Americans like himself systematically hoisted glasses on the way to the ruin, moral or physical or both, that besets so many of them now. More spectacularly, it is places of decadent entertainment like the Casino where the naked Negro dancer Josephine Baker performs "her chocolate arabesques." It is squalidly visible along the streets of Montmartre, the Rue Pigalle and the Place Blanche, where night-clubs like "the two great mouths of the Café of Heaven and the Café of Hell" used to wait, as they still do, to devour busloads of tourists, innocent foreigners eager for a glimpse of Parisian fleshpots.

Fittingly enough, it is in the Ritz bar that the story opens—and closes. The place is nothing like it used to be. A stillness, "strange and portentous," inhabits the handsome room. No longer can it be thought of as an American bar: it has "gone back into France." All the former habitués are absent—Campbell ailing in Switzerland; Hardt back at work in the United States; and Fessenden, who tried to pass a bad check to the management, wrecked at last by shame and obesity. Only Duncan Schaeffer is still around Paris. Swallowing his loneliness, Charlie Wales hands the assistant bartender a note for Schaeffer including the address of his brother-in-law in the Rue Palatine. It is his first mistake. A key clicks in the prison door. Although he does not know it yet, Schaeffer will twice seek Charlie out, only to lock him into loneliness again.

At the outset Fitzgerald alternates interior and exterior scenes, with the obvious intent of providing the Babylonian background against which the principal dramatic scenes are to occur. While Charlie is on his way to the Peters's apartment in the Rue Palatine, he is most impressed by the nocturnal beauty rather than the wickedness of Paris. Bistros gleam like jewels along the boulevards, and the "fire-red, gas-blue, ghost-green signs" blur their way "smokily through the tranquil rain." By contrast, the living room at his brother-in-law's place is "warm and comfortably American," with a fire on the hearth and a pleasant domestic bustle in the kitchen. Although Honoria is well, and happy enough with her small cousins, she is plainly overjoyed to see her father again. At dinner he watches her closely, wondering whom she most resembles, himself or her mother. It will be fortunate, he thinks, "if she didn't combine the traits of both that had brought them to disaster."

—Carlos Baker, "When the Story Ends: 'Babylon Revisited,'" *The Short Stories of F. Scott Fitzgerald: New Approaches in Criticism*, ed. Jackson R. Bryer (Madison: University of Wisconsin Press, 1982): pp. 270–271.

ELSA NETTELS ON THE MOTHER-GUARDIAN FIGURE

[Elsa Nettels has taught at the College of William and Mary and has published widely in American literature. In this excerpt from her essay "Howells's 'A Circle in the Water' and Fitzgerald's 'Babylon Revisited,'" she compares the two authors' use of the mother-guardian figure to articulate the story's primary moral crisis.]

Fitzgerald is also linked with Howells by the striking resemblances of his story "Babylon Revisited" (1931) to Howells's story "A Circle in the Water," first published in *Scribner's Magazine* in 1895 and collected in the volume of Howells's short stories *A Pair of Patient Lovers*, published by Harper's in 1901 and by Tauchnitz in 1905....

"A Circle of Water" and "Babylon Revisited" both center on a middle-aged man whose wife is dead and who through folly or crime has lost custody of his only child, a daughter. . . . Each story beings with the man's return after an absence of months or years to the city where his daughter lives with her guardians—Boston in Howells's story, Paris in Fitzgerald's. Tedham desires from his sister-in-law and her husband, the Haskeths, permission to see his daughter Fay, now age eighteen, in hope of being reunited with her. Charlie Wales supplicates his sister-in-law, Marion Peters, and her husband Lincoln, in hopes of regaining custody of his nine-year-old daughter, Honoria. Both fathers see reunion with their daughters as the sign that they have paid the price demanded by others and fully atoned for their wrongs....

In both stories, the irregular past life of the father is contrasted with the sober, conventional, well-regulated household of the child's guardians. . . . The sister-in-law of the returned exile is the chief source of the distrust and hatred he suffers. . . . Marion Peters regards her brother-in-law with "unalterable distrust," speaks to him coldly and looks at him with "hard eyes." She too, disapproved of her sister's marriage. "She had lived for a long time with a prejudice—a prejudice founded on the curious disbelief in her sister's happiness, and which, in the shock of one terrible night, had turned to hatred for him." Mrs. Hasketh's dislike of Tedham seems born of her distrust of his character; Marion Peters's hatred of Charlie Wales springs in part from her envy of his wealth, but both women reveal their need to explain and justify themselves, insisting that the father's collapse forced them to intervene and that they act solely in the child's interest. Both women appear overwrought, given to nervous illness which they can use as a weapon against the child's father. Hasketh says of his wife, "She is never very strong," and she confesses to the Marches that "the sight of Mr. Tedham would make me sick." After Duncan and Lorraine have gone, Lincoln Peters explains to

Charlie, "Marion's not well and she can't stand shocks. That kind of people make her really physically sick." . . .

The central question in each story is raised by the sister-in-law. . . . The daughter in "Babylon Revisited" is too young to determine her future; she is essentially a passive figure, last seen being swung like a pendulum by her uncle. The central question concerns not her but her father. Will he be a responsible guardian of his daughter or will he lapse again into dissipation? "How long are you going to stay sober, Charlie?" Marion Peters asks her brother-in-law, making her duty to Honoria dependent upon her judgment of Charlie, which only time can vindicate. Charlie's refusal to take a second drink at the end of the story when he sits alone in the bar with his shattered hopes suggests that he may, as he says, stay sober "permanently," but Marion's question, "How can anybody count on that?" cannot be conclusively answered. Her view of Charlie is clearly prejudiced and yet her mistrust may be justifiable. The divergence of opinion among readers—some arguing that Charlie Wales is truly reformed, others arguing that he is essentially unchanged or is divided by conflicting desires—shows that, unlike "A Circle in the Water," Fitzgerald's story does not render final judgment of the characters or reveal the ultimate effects of their actions. In both stories, a woman's feeling determines the outcome, but in Howells's story the decisive force is love, which brings Tedham's punishment to an end; in Fitzgerald's story the decisive force is hate, which leaves the reader to wonder whether Charlie will be forced to "pay forever."

Elsa Nettels, "Howells's 'A Circle in the Water' and Fitzgerald's 'Babylon Revisited,'" *Studies in Short Fiction* 19 (Summer 1982): pp. 262–265.

Plot Summary of
"Crazy Sunday"

"Crazy Sunday" appeared in *The American Mercury* in October 1932 and was later collected in *Taps at Reveille* (1935). This tightly constructed psychological drama is set in Hollywood in the early 1930s. More than just a setting, Hollywood's theatrical ambiance provides one of Fitzgerald's primary subjects in the story. In particular, he probes the artistic potential that such an atmosphere offers. In a place where life and art are so intertwined, the difference between reality and its imitation becomes almost impossible to recognize—a situation dangerously akin to madness, as the story's title suggests. By portraying the interactions of three characters (all masters in the business of make-believe), Fitzgerald represents the overlap between art, illusion, and self-deception.

Many critics have explored the connection between the events in "Crazy Sunday" and Fitzgerald's own experiences in Hollywood. He wrote the story after working on a screenplay in Hollywood during the winter of 1931. He transformed personal events (including an inebriated, humiliating impromptu performance of his song "Dog" at a tea party given by a famous Hollywood couple) into fiction. Such analysis and speculation seem appropriate in relation to "Crazy Sunday" because the story seeks to represent the blurry line between reality and artistic expression.

When Joel Coles walks with Stella Calman in the glow of his attraction for her, his emotion transforms the world into a stage set for love. As he walks on that stage, however, he remains fully aware of the illusion his desire has created. Like his colleagues in the movie business, Joel has been behind the scenes enough to know that nothing is real, no matter how appealing it seems. "There were Christmas trees already in the shop windows and the full moon over the boulevard was only a prop, as scenic as the giant boudoir lamps of the corners." Even the moon is a stage prop—if it hadn't existed, someone would have invented it, and hung it up for its effect.

In such an environment, both artistic and moral integrity become compromised. Joel Coles, the protagonist, illuminates the double bind that the Hollywood atmosphere creates: "He [refers] to himself modestly as a hack but really [does] not think of it that way." In other words, he thinks his writing has meaning and merit. In his own mind, he is not a pretender to talent or to love of his craft—he has both. In spite of that, he has to dissemble, and calls himself a "hack," a fake. In this, Coles resembles Fitzgerald, who like Mark Twain, often disparaged his writing—particularly his short stories, as opposed to his novels—as hack work, written quickly for money. Like Joel Coles, Fitzgerald no doubt struck this pose for complicated reasons.

Joel recognizes a superior artistic integrity in Miles Calman, "an artist from the top of his curiously shaped head to his niggerish feet." (As Sheldon Grebstein insightfully points out, Fitzgerald's racialized description of Calman draws on stereotypes of the time that associated both Jews and African Americans with entertainment and show business.) Miles seems to be the genuine article, even in his physical appearance. But as the story unfolds, and as Joel gains a closer understanding of Miles, he too seems to be in the grips of self-delusion. He has been performing an elaborate charade, having an affair with his wife's best friend in the limelight of their own domestic circle. His professional control over his films contrasts with his lack of control over his personal actions. He seems remorseful about his infidelity but powerless to stop it. He hopes that psycho-analysis will help him uncover the unconscious fantasies that are interfering with his life and ruining his marriage. ("The psychoana-lyst told Miles that he had a mother complex. In his first marriage he transferred his mother complex to his wife, you see—and then his sex turned to me," Stella explains. "But when we married the thing repeated itself—he transferred his mother complex to me and all his libido turned toward this other woman.")

In Hollywood, life and illusion are inextricably bound. The Cal-mans' private tragedy seems contrived for an audience, and their house deliberately "built for great emotional moments." As Stella raves on to him about her discovery of Miles's affair, Joel realizes that he does "not quite believe in picture actresses' grief." He won-ders about the sincerity of Stella's role as a wounded wife; for him, "she [seems to hover] somewhere between the realest of realities and the most blatant of impersonations." Meanwhile, "he [pretends] to listen and instead [thinks] how well she was got up." We increasingly trust Joel's observations, but he too plays roles—the faithful friend, the concerned listener. Fitzgerald's emphasis on acts of looking and visual appearances creates a hall of mirrors wherein the desire to see and know is pitted against the ubiquitous fact that looks are deceiving.

The public unraveling of the Calman marriage provides a topos that Fitzgerald returns to again and again in his fiction—in *The Great Gatsby,* in *Tender Is the Night,* and in several other short stories. His fascination with marital difficulties undoubtedly arose from his personal experiences; he rearranged and transmuted material from life to create a tightly crafted fiction.

In "Crazy Sunday," as the title indicates, all the major actions take place on a succession of three Sundays. On both the first and the third Sundays, Miles is largely absent, but the idea of him dominates the minds of Stella and Joel. Like Jay Gatsby, Miles Calman makes a somewhat shadowy hero, and much of the story's interest lies in Joel's development vis-à-vis Miles, rather than in Miles himself. This narrative split emphasizes the essentially theatrical nature of the Calmans' conflict. In other words, this story explores how a conflict between two people—a husband and wife—is continually played out in relation to a third person, either Joel or Eva Goebel. In this it resembles art, and in particular dramatic art, which is always contrived and performed for an audience. The Calmans seem to enjoy the dramatic possibilities of their situation, and the publicity of their disagreements gives them a greater importance, the air of tragedy.

At the end of the story, after the news of Miles's death has stirred Stella's enthusiastic desperation, Joel realizes that she wants to keep him there in order "to keep Miles alive by sustaining a situation in which he had figured." She needs him there so that she can continue to play the role of Miles's wife. Without an audience, her identity and her connection to the man she loved will not be visible and will seem less real. Although Joel seems masterful and decisive in his refusal to play along with Stella's fantasy, the story ends with his grim prophecy, "Oh, yes, I'll be back—I'll be back!"

In the end, as in so many of Fitzgerald works, a dream has gone out of the world and been lost. Miles's artistic integrity will never return. As Joel leaves Miles's home, he recognizes that what Miles created is already starting to disintegrate: "What a hell of a hole he leaves in this damn wilderness—already!" ❀

List of Characters in
"Crazy Sunday"

Joel Coles, the son of a famous actress, writes "continuity" for one of the big motion picture studios. He retains some integrity, which Hollywood does not foster. The story represents him during his ascent: he is poised for a successful career, although there is a grim prophecy in the observation that he is "not yet broken by Hollywood." The grueling studio work schedule does not leave Joel much time for leisure or private life; on Sundays, he finds himself improvising an identity. Although he thinks he has few illusions left, he manages to lose some in the course of the story.

Miles Calman is the story's tragic hero. He is the real artist—"the only American-born director with both an interesting temperament and an artistic conscience." He has a successful career in Hollywood and can direct his movies without having to truckle to studio executives and producers. His artistic integrity has produced a few "experimental flops" but not a single "cheap picture." His personal life, in contrast, is compromised by jealousy, intrigue, and infidelity. He "has the unhappiest eyes Joel ever saw."

Stella Walker Calman is the wife of Miles Calman. She has easy grace and charm, and Joel finds himself falling in love with her. A talented actress, she instinctively recognizes the dramatic possibilities in everyday life and plays her part to the hilt. She wears little makeup and has a natural look. "She [hovers] somewhere between the realest of realities and the most blatant of impersonations." Joel wants to talk with her "as if she were a girl instead of a name"—she goes back and forth between the two. She seems genuinely in love with her husband and hurt by his infidelity with her friend, Eva Goebel, but Joel can never be sure where her acting begins.

Nat Keogh, another studio writer, is a minor character in the story and a foil for Joel Coles. He drinks to excess and no longer has Joel's youth or good looks. He represents what Joel might become. ❀

Critical Views on
"Crazy Sunday"

T. S. MATTHEWS ON FITZGERALD AND WRITING

[In this 1935 review of *Taps at Reveille*, the collection of stories that contained "Crazy Sunday" and "Babylon Revisited," T. S. Matthews expresses a typical understanding of the split between novels and short stories. This view oriented most commentary on Fitzgerald until the 1960s.]

Scott Fitzgerald is supposed to be a case of split personality: Fitzgerald A is the serious writer; Fitzgerald B brings home the necessary bacon. And *Taps at Reveille*, a collection of avowed potboilers, was written with his fingers crossed by Fitzgerald B. There seems to be a feeling abroad that it would be kinder not to take any critical notice of the goings-on of Fitzgerald B, since his better half is such a superior person and might be embarrassed. Mr. Fitzgerald himself, however, obviously doesn't feel that way about it, for he signs his moniker to all and sundry, and even collects the offerings of his lower nature in a book. He is right: there is no real difference in kind between *Taps at Reveille* and *Tender Is the Night;* the creatures whom he has sold down the river for a good price are a little cruder, that's all. The yearning toward maturity is even more noticeable in some of these short stories than it is in his novels. It used to seem awful to Mr. Fitzgerald that youth should have to become manhood; now it seems even more awful that it can't. His heroes have grown older but not riper; in their middle thirties they are hurt and puzzled children, lost among their contemporary elders, and still longing to grow up.

—T. S. Matthews, untitled review of *Taps at Reveille* in *The New Republic* 98 (1935): p. 108.

ELLEN MOERS ON FITZGERALD AND HOLLYWOOD

[Ellen Moers (1928–1979) was a professor and literary critic. Her books include *Two Dreisers* and *Literary Women*. In these excerpts from her article "F. Scott Fitzgerald: Reveille at Taps," she distinguishes Fitzgerald's penchant for autobiography in the stories as opposed to the novels, and traces Fitzgerald's fascination with Hollywood.]

The gold in F. Scott Fitzgerald lies in his short stories, and they should be mined. He wrote about one hundred and sixty of them, half of which have never been reprinted from the magazines in which they originally appeared. In the atmosphere of tender regret engendered by Andrew Turnbull's graceful biographical tribute, much satisfaction has been voiced over our own ability to worship Fitzgerald when our distant ancestors of the 1940s ignored him. It might be sobering to reflect that we still do not know, and thus can hardly evaluate his work.

Fitzgerald looks very different when regarded primarily as a short story writer and secondarily as a novelist. He looks better, too. Nothing, I imagine, will unseat *The Great Gatsby,* in critical opinion and popular reception, as the finest thing Fitzgerald wrote. It is also by far the shortest of his novels and, in terms of the span of years covered in the life of its main character, more compressed than many of his stories. [...]

The Fitzgerald of the short stories, including *The Great Gatsby,* is one of the least egotistical of authors. When he draws himself as the protagonist of a novel, self-disgust, shame, guilt, in short the failure to make himself a hero, cast an embarrassing pall over the whole book. When he puts himself into a short story, he figures as the naive, the weak, the incompetent but utterly attractive and characteristically American innocent. The narrators of *Gatsby,* of "The Rich Boy," of "A Short Trip Home," of "The Last of the Belles," have the short end of the stick, but wave it with extraordinary grace. "At twenty-three," says one of them for all of them, "I was utterly unconvinced about anything, except that some people were strong and attractive and could do what they wanted, and others were caught and disgraced. I hoped I was one of the former." The statement poses one of the two great themes in Fitzgerald's work: power as an emanation of personality and, conversely, the pains and pleasures, above all the survival, of the weak. The other theme was Love, which Fitzgerald seemed to believe was something the powerful inspired and the weak felt.

Fitzgerald may have paid little attention to the great cosmopolitan experiments in the arts that fascinated and influenced his fellow American expatriates during their years in France, but he did not miss the movies. In his way he was the chronicler of the Movie Age, with its brilliance and stupidity, its splashing generosity and its petty cruelties, its creation of art and its waste of talent, its laughable artificiality and its emotional power. The impossibly gorgeous décor of "The Diamond as Big as the Ritz" (1922) springs from the imagination of "a moving picture fella"; after an architect, a decadent poet, and a stage designer had gone mad over the assignment, "he was the only man we found who was used to playing with an unlimited amount of money, though he did tuck his napkin in his collar and couldn't read or write." The nemesis of *The Beautiful and Damned* (1922) is Joseph Bloeckman, the sinister Jew who, in the course of his rise from immigrant peanut vendor to movie magnate ("as always, infinitesimally improved, of subtler intonation, of more convincing ease") dazzles the beautiful Gloria with the temptation of becoming a star. Something of the childish spirit of Gatsby's parties (1925) is imported from Hollywood, along with some of the guests. Fitzgerald wrote two good stories about Hollywood people after his first working trip there (in 1927) and one excellent story, "Crazy Sunday," after his second trip (in 1931). The stunning opening section of *Tender Is the Night* (1934) deals with the reactions of a young Hollywood star. And, of course, *The Last Tycoon*—Fitzgerald's unfinished, perhaps most ambitious novel—was written in, about and for Hollywood, where he lived most of his last three years.

—Ellen Moers, "F. Scott Fitzgerald: Reveille at Taps," *Commentary* 34, no. 12 (December 1962): pp. 526–530.

KENNETH EBLE ON REAL-LIFE EVENTS IN "CRAZY SUNDAY"

[Kenneth Eble teaches at the University of Utah. His books include *The Profane Comedy* (1962) and *F. Scott Fitzgerald* (1963). He is coeditor of *The Craft of Teaching* (1976). In this excerpt from his article "Touches of Disaster: Alcoholism and Mental Illness in Fitzgerald's Short Stories," he explores the real-life events that Fitzgerald transformed in the story.]

Fitzgerald's best-known Hollywood story, "Crazy Sunday" (1932), reveals both the actuality of Fitzgerald's drinking and his masquerading of it in his fiction. The incident behind the story was a party given by Irving Thalberg—later the model for Monroe Stahr in *The Last Tycoon*—and Norma Shearer. According to Dwight Taylor, a fellow writer at MGM who accompanied him to the party, Fitzgerald got drunk, insulted Robert Montgomery, and insisted on singing a banal song about a dog. The song embarrassed everyone, though Norma Shearer sent Fitzgerald a telegram the next day: "I thought you were one of the most agreeable persons at our tea," which Fitzgerald used almost word for word in the story. At the end of the week he was fired. In his fictionalizing of the story, Fitzgerald described Joel Coles, the drunken writer, in such a way as to be identified with Taylor and gave himself the role of the writer who tried to save him. No perceptive reader of Fitzgerald's stories is likely to be fooled, for the central character clearly betrays the conscience, guilt, moralizing, and defiance with which Fitzgerald viewed his drinking.

—Kenneth E. Eble, "Touches of Disaster: Alcoholism and Mental Illness in Fitzgerald's Short Stories," in *The Short Stories of F. Scott Fitzgerald: New Approaches in Criticism,* ed. Jackson R. Bryer. (Madison: University of Wisconsin Press, 1982): pp. 44–45.

[Sheldon Grebstein has been president of the State University of New York at Purchase and has taught at the State University of New York at Binghamton. He is the author of *Hemingway's Craft* and has contributed essays to several journals. In this excerpt from his article "'The Sane Method of 'Crazy Sunday,'" he identifies the story's main theme: beauty's reciprocal relation to its opposite, destruction.]

As its most obvious theme or subject, "Crazy Sunday" contrasts the physical beauty, charisma, or talent of its major characters—Joel, Stella, Miles—with the element of instability, weakness, or tendency toward self-destruction which seems to coincide, even be necessary, to their beauty and talent. Joel drinks to excess. Miles is exhausted, marked for death. The alluring Stella is emotionally fragile, subject to hysteria. What Joel first says to Stella as a conversational gambit— "Everybody's afraid, aren't they?"—becomes a portentous cue to this dimension of character.

The story's atmosphere and action are thus intensely psychological, not only in the specifically psychiatric sense conveyed in Miles's talk of his psychoanalysis and personal troubles, but more important in that the narrative emphasizes states of feeling and the impressions people make upon one another from moment to moment. In this, Fitzgerald expresses his vision of one aspect of the Hollywood milieu which differentiates it from the run of common life: there the most private matters—marital infidelity, sexual problems—are discussed as though they were public knowledge. Relationships that would take months, even years, to develop in "real" or "normal" life are accelerated, foreshortened, developed in one or two brief encounters. In this concentration and distillation of experience, Fitzgerald both exercises the economy of the short story form and evokes the method of a film scenario. [...]

Appropriately, the emphasis on the psychological dimension is reinforced by the story's dramatic structure. This structure basically depends not upon the five formal sections into which Fitzgerald has overtly divided it, although these are important as phases in the action, but upon three crazy Sundays. In turn, each of these Sundays serves as the occasion for the exposure and humiliation of each of the main characters.

—Sheldon Grebstein, "The Sane Method of 'Crazy Sunday,'" in *The Short Stories of F. Scott Fitzgerald: New Approaches in Criticism,* ed. Jackson R. Bryer (Madison: University of Wisconsin Press, 1982): pp. 280–281.

Works by
F. Scott Fitzgerald

Fie! Fie! Fi-Fi! 1914.

The Evil Eye. 1915.

Safety First. 1916.

This Side of Paradise. 1921.

Flappers and Philosophers. 1920.

The Beautiful and Damned. 1922.

Tales of the Jazz Age. 1922.

The Vegetable. 1923.

The Great Gatsby. 1925.

All the Sad Young Men. 1926.

John Jackson's Arcady (arranged for reading by Lilian Holmes Strack). 1928.

Tender Is the Night. 1934.

Taps at Reveille. 1935.

The Last Tycoon. 1941.

The Crack-Up, ed. Edmund Wilson. 1945.

The Stories of F. Scott Fitzgerald, ed. Malcolm Cowley. 1951.

Afternoon of an Author, ed. Arthur Mizener. 1957.

The Pat Hobby Stories, ed. Arnold Gingrich. 1962.

The Letters of F. Scott Fitzgerald, ed. Andrew Turnbull. 1963.

The Apprentice Fiction of F. Scott Fitzgerald, ed. John Kuehl. 1965.

Thoughtbook of Francis Scott Key Fitzgerald, ed. John Kuehl. 1965.

Dearly Beloved. 1970.

F. Scott Fitzgerald in His Own Time: A Miscellany, ed. 1971.

Dear Scott/Dear Max, ed. John Kuehl and Jackson R. Bryer. 1971.

As Ever, Scott Fitz—, ed. Matthew J. Bruccoli and Jennifer M. Atkinson. 1972.

The Basil and Josephine Stories, ed. Jackson R. Bryer and John Kuehl. 1973.

F. Scott Fitzgerald's Ledger (A Facsimile), ed. Matthew J. Bruccoli. 1973.

Bits of Paradise, ed. Matthew J. Bruccoli and Scottie Fitzgerald Smith. 1973.

Preface to This Side of Paradise. 1975.

The Cruise of the Rolling Junk. 1976.

F. Scott Fitzgerald's Screenplay for Eric Maria Remarque's Three Comrades, ed. Matthew J. Bruccoli. 1978.

The Notebooks of F. Scott Fitzgerald, ed. Matthew J. Bruccoli. 1978.

F. Scott Fitzgerald's St. Paul Plays, ed. Alan Margolies. 1978.

The Price Was High, ed. Matthew J. Bruccoli. 1979.

Correspondence of F. Scott Fitzgerald, ed. Matthew J. Bruccoli and Margaret M. Duggan, with Susan Walker. 1980.

Poems 1911–1940, ed. Matthew J. Bruccoli. 1981.

The Short Stories of F. Scott Fitzgerald: A New Collection, ed. Matthew J. Bruccoli. 1989.

Works about
F. Scott Fitzgerald

Allen, Joan M. *Candles and Carnival Lights: The Catholic Sensibility of F. Scott Fitzgerald.* New York: New York University Press, 1978.

Bigsby, C. W. E. "The Two Identities of F. Scott Fitzgerald," in *The American Novel and the Nineteen Twenties.* London: Edward Arnold, 1971.

Bloom, Harold, ed. *Modern Critical Views: F. Scott Fitzgerald.* New York: Chelsea House, 1985.

Bruccoli, Matthew J. *Some Sort of Epic Grandeur: The Life of F. Scott Fitzgerald.* New York: Harcourt Brace Jovanovich, 1981.

Bryer, Jackson R., ed. *F. Scott Fitzgerald: The Critical Reception.* New York: Burt Franklin, 1978.

Bryer, Jackson R., ed. *New Essays on F. Scott Fitzgerald's Neglected Stories.* Columbia and London: University of Missouri Press, 1996.

Claridge, Henry, ed. *F. Scott Fitzgerald: Critical Assessments.* The Banks, East Sussex: Helm Information Ltd., 1991.

Cross, K. G. W. *F. Scott Fitzgerald.* Edinburgh: Oliver and Boyd, 1964; New York: Grove Press, 1964.

Eble, Kenneth. *F. Scott Fitzgerald.* Revised Edition. Twayne's United States Authors Series, No. 36. Boston: Twayne, 1977.

Eble, Kenneth E., ed. *F. Scott Fitzgerald: A Collection of Criticism.* New York: McGraw-Hill, 1973.

Fiedler, Leslie. "Some Notes on F. Scott Fitzgerald," in *An End to Innocence.* Boston: Beacon Press, 1955, pp. 174–182.

Gallo, Rose Adrienne. *F. Scott Fitzgerald.* New York: Frederick Ungar, 1978.

Geismar, Maxwell. "F. Scott Fitzgerald: Orestes at the Ritz," in *The Last of the Provincials.* Boston: Houghton Mifflin, 1943, pp. 287–352.

Goldburst, William. *F. Scott Fitzgerald and His Contemporaries.* Cleveland: World, 1963.

Higgins, John A. *F. Scott Fitzgerald: A Study of the Stories.* Jamaica, N.Y.: St. John's University Press, 1971.

Hindus, Milton. *F. Scott Fitzgerald: An Introduction and Interpretation.* New York: Holt, Rinehart and Winston, 1968.

Hoffman, Frederick J., ed. *"The Great Gatsby": A Study.* New York: Charles Scribner's, 1962.

Kazin, Alfred, ed. *F. Scott Fitzgerald: The Man and His Work.* Cleveland: World, 1951.

Kazin, Alfred. *On Native Grounds.* New York: Reynal and Hitchcock, 1942.

Latham, Aaron. *Crazy Sundays: F. Scott Fitzgerald in Hollywood.* New York: Viking Press, 1971.

Lehan, Richard D. *F. Scott Fitzgerald and the Craft of Fiction.* Carbondale: Southern Illinois University Press, 1966.

Long, Robert Emmet. *The Achieving of "The Great Gatsby": F. Scott Fitzgerald, 1920–1925.* Lewisburg, Pa.: Bucknell University Press, 1979.

Miller, James E., Jr. *F. Scott Fitzgerald: His Art and His Technique.* New York: New York University Press, 1964.

Mizener, Arthur. *The Far Side of Paradise: A Biography of F. Scott Fitzgerald.* Revised Edition. Boston: Houghton Mifflin, 1965.

Mizener, Arthur, ed. *F. Scott Fitzgerald: A Collection of Critical Essays.* Englewood Cliffs, N.J.: Prentice-Hall, 1963.

Perosa, Sergio. *The Art of F. Scott Fitzgerald.* Translated by Charles Metz and Sergio Perosa. Ann Arbor: University of Michigan Press, 1965.

Petry, Alice Hall. *Fitzgerald's Craft of Short Fiction: The Collected Stories 1920–1935.* Studies in Modern Literature, No. 103. Ann Arbor: UMI Research Press, 1989.

Piper, Henry Dan. *F. Scott Fitzgerald: A Critical Portrait.* New York: Holt, Rinehart and Winston, 1965.

Roulston, Robert and Helen H. *The Winding Road to West Egg: The Artistic Development of F. Scott Fitzgerald.* London: Associated University Presses, 1995.

Shain, Charles E. *F. Scott Fitzgerald.* University of Minnesota Pamphlets on American Writers, No. 15. Minneapolis: University of Minnesota Press, 1961.

Sklar, Robert. *F. Scott Fitzgerald: The Last Laocoön.* New York: Oxford University Press, 1967.

Stanley, Linda C. *The Foreign Critical Reception of F. Scott Fitzgerald: An Analysis and Annotated Bibliography*. Westport, Conn.: Greenwood Press, 1980.

Untermeyer, Louis. "F. Scott Fitzgerald," in *Makers of the Modern World*. New York: Simon and Schuster, 1955.

Way, Brian. *F. Scott Fitzgerald and the Art of Social Fiction*. London: Edward Arnold, 1980; New York: St Martin's, 1980.

Wells, Walter. "The Hero and the Hack," in *Tycoons and Locusts: A Regional Look at Hollywood Fiction of the 1930s*. Carbondale: Southern Illinois University Press, 1973.

West, James L. W. III. *The Making of F. Scott Fitzgerald's "This Side of Paradise."* Columbia, S.C.: J. Faust, 1977.

Index of
Themes and Ideas